COLLISION
AVOIDANCE

Staying Alive in the
National Airspace

Victor R. Beaver

Visual Flight Rules &

Instrument Flight Procedures

Explained

ISBN-13 978-1086221398

Published in the United States of America

Special Note

Pertaining to the content of this book, I intended no ill will toward those civilian aviation companies I worked for throughout my flying career. Rocky Mountain Helicopters, Ballard Aviation, Air Methods, and Metro Aviation, each I have and will always have the highest regard for their training methods, their care and concern for their employees, their desire to always deal with the persons associated with their contracts in a professional manner consistent with sound aviation practices. Each aviation entity by regulation was and is sanctioned by the Federal Aviation Administration. Suffice to say we EMS pilots were forever under the watchful eye of hospital administrators, the FAA, chief pilots, and medical crewmembers, seemingly never a moment went by that wasn't fraught with peril and pitfall. Safe, collision-free flying to those still in the game. As my dad used to say: "Keep her low and slow." I never did know what he meant by that.

I dedicate this work to my dad,

Victor H. Beaver,

who spent

many, many hours in the cockpit …

"W0YB"

USAF CW2 Retired

August 5, 1922 – December 4, 2001

"Howdy. Haven't we met before?"

"Not like this."

When two or more pilots take to the skies at the same time in the same area, they are likely to conflict if they don't follow the guidelines spelled out in the current FAR/AIM. This book has been written to explain the reasoning behind those rules and procedures that all pilots must be familiar with if they are to return safely to home and hearth.

Table of Contents

Part One—Visual Flight Rules Explained

Part Two—Instrument Flight Procedures Explained

Table of Contents (cont.)

*Note: The FAR/AIM 2020 was used as reference in the preparation of this book. Also, in that powered parachute and weight-shift-control aircraft are unlikely to be used for an instrument approach procedure, I refer only to the use of the helicopter and airplane for all aspects of flight in the national airspace.

Forward

THE SUBJECT of this book is *understanding visual flight rules and instrument flight procedures* as they pertain to the national airspace. The theme is collision avoidance. I spent 38 years as a professional helicopter pilot. I retired July 2008. A helicopter pilot has 21 lives; I had used up 37 of mine.

I joined the U.S. Army in 1965 never intending to be a pilot. One day while pondering my future as a paratrooper with the 82nd Airborne Division at Fort Bragg, North Carolina, someone mentioned "why don't you go to helicopter flight training?" I asked how old I had to be. "Eighteen." I was eighteen. "How much college do I need?" I was told no college, just a high school diploma. I had one of those. From then on, as I anticipated  my class date to attend the Army's warrant officer candidate flight training program, I watched with near breathless amazement every time a UH-1 "Huey" helicopter landed near the buildings where I worked. It was such an incredible flying machine, the workhorse of the Vietnam war. From my vantage point, I couldn't see either pilot in the cockpit. What kind of person flies a helicopter as a career? What magic wizardry made the thing go up and down?

 My pilot training began at Fort Wolters, Texas, January 1967, along with 450 other training hopefuls. September 23, 1967, I received my coveted silver aviator wings. One month later I was a brand-new warrant officer pilot assigned to the 121st Assault Helicopter Company, Soc Trang, South Vietnam, deep in the Mekong Delta.

Flight school academics was presented in such a helter-skelter way it's a wonder I retained any of it. Though I was reasonably equipped to be an army pilot, I was woefully inadequate to carry that knowledge into the nonmilitary arena ... when I attempted to acquire my first civilian job. FAA rules and procedures are sacrosanct. Army rules and procedures, when applied to war, can be adjusted to suit the situation — or disregarded altogether.

I hated instrument training. With that damn hood somewhat blocking my forward vision, and with all my peripheral vision gone (which hampered completely my ability to think), I stumbled through that portion of my training certain I was an "instrument pilot" misfit. Besides, what army asks its pilots to make an instrument assault into a fogged-in landing zone. Thankfully, we were never tasked to do that.

I was released from active duty March 1970. I attended college for two years, and at the same time became fixed-wing rated. After a fashion I joined the Utah Army National Guard, then became a member of the Colorado Army National Guard until my request for recall to active duty came through. During this time the Army needed experienced pilots to fill the instructor-pilot ranks at Fort Rucker, Alabama, the main aviator training center. Lo and behold I became an instrument flight instructor. For nine years I taught in-strument flight procedures to rated stu-dent aviators and army student pilots. To teach, they say, is to learn twice. Did I ever.

SA 316B Allouette III

In 1988, I left Fort Rucker and went to work as a "flight for life" EMS helicop-ter pilot for Rocky Mountain Helicopters headquartered at Provo, Utah. My first duty assignment (as a relief pilot) was John-stown, Pennsylvania, after which I was sent to Louisville, Kentucky. I found a per-manent home for the next five years in Springfield, Missouri. After a six-year hia-tus, having endured an unfortunate personal incident that caused me to move on, I returned to EMS flying in the year 2000. I wandered from St. Joseph, Missouri, to Joplin, Missouri, then to Destin, Florida, to Branson West, Missouri, finally ending up in Harlingen, Texas, near Brownsville and the border.

When a request for service came over the paging system, crew and pilot where usually airborne within five to seven minutes. Often, we had no idea where we were going, or which hospital we had to go to once a patient was onboard. It was imperative to continually monitor the weather and to decide before a call came in

MBB BO 105

where I could and couldn't go based on the mini-mum weather requirements dictated by my com-pany. Aside from using an aeronautical chart, I also carried and referenced a state road map. This map provided highway numbers and intersec-tions not typically displayed on a regular flying chart. We had GPS, but receiving the right set of coordinates depended on several factors: how well, for example, the calling (requesting) agency could relay its position to the dis-patcher and how well the dispatcher could translate their position into a set of co-ordinates, to include using the right lat/long format. Going to a highway accident at night was generally the easiest, as the emergency flashers of police, firefighter, and ambulance crew vehicles were visible from several miles away. Not only was

I well versed in VFR flying, I had to remind myself how easy it was to get into tight weather situations needing my skill and expertise as an instrument-rated pilot.

During my time as an EMS pilot I had many opportunities to ferry aircraft from point A to point B, each flight performed solo. I ferried aircraft from Provo, Utah, to West Chester, Pennsylvania; from Destin, Florida, to Shreveport, Louisiana; from Huntington, West Virginia, to Joplin, Missouri; from Provo, Utah, to Springfield, Missouri; from Johnstown, Pennsylvania, to Louisville, Kentucky;

Eurocopter EC 135

from Albuquerque, New Mexico, to Joplin, Missouri; from Olathe, Kansas, to Colorado Springs; from Traverse City, Michigan, to Harlingen, Texas, so on and so forth. Each flight was an opportunity to challenge the weather without concern for medical crew or patient. I had my VFR sectional chart(s) folded just right. I kept myself oriented using VORs and NDBs and broadcast stations and prominent landmarks. I followed major highways when convenient; and I used my GPS receiver. After each fuel stop, I filed a new VFR flight plan per company policy, made position reports to FSS (flight service station), and received weather reports whenever I could. It was the least stressful flying I had ever done. I enjoyed every minute of it.

TH-55A Trainer

Over the course of my career, I became qualified in a variety of military and civilian aircraft: the UH-1 "Huey" helicopter, the OH-6A "Cayuse" scout helicopter, the Hughes 269 "TH-55A" training helicopter; and then in the civilian world: the SA 316B "Allouette III," the German-built MBB BO 105, the Eurocopter EC 135, the AS 350 "AStar", and the AS 355 "TwinStar" F and N models. I had more "numbers" and separate emergency procedures running through my head than Carter has liver pills. EMS flying was a lively sport. I relate all this to support the idea that I might know what I'm talking about.

It is my desire to present the material herein logically, from concept to concept, each new concept built upon the previous one, in hierarchal order. An ordered mind is an ordered cockpit.

The reader is expected to have a current FAR/AIM as reference. Since the FAR/AIM is time sensitive, it is my hope that the explanations I give are general enough to compensate for minor changes and possibly those that are major. If nothing else, this book should help you think more clearly about flight in the national airspace. Collision avoidance is the subject throughout the book. It is not for me to nitpick those rules or procedures that do not promote this theme.

So, buckle up, sit back and enjoy. I guarantee that regardless your flight hours or experience you will gain something useful out of this book well worth the expense.

October 18, 1967 — October 18, 1968
Soc Trang and Vinh Long (IV Corps)

First Cavalry
Division (Airmobile)

INFANT NEIT
(Iroquois Night Fighter
and
Night Tracker)

October 26, 1969 — December 27, 1969
Lai Khe (III Corps)

Part One

Visual Flight Rules
Explained

"AS 350 AStar Écureuil"

Introduction

(Excerpt from the National Transportation Safety Board report.)

ON JULY 16, 1999, John F. Kennedy Jr. died when the airplane he was piloting crashed into the Atlantic Ocean off the coast of Martha's Vineyard, Massachusetts. The two passengers on board, Kennedy's wife Carolyn Bessette and her sister Lauren, were also killed. The Piper Saratoga light aircraft had departed from Essex County Airport in Fairfield, New Jersey. Kennedy's intended route was along the coastline of Connecticut and across Rhode Island Sound to the Martha's Vineyard airport.

Piper Saratoga

The official investigation by the National Transportation Safety Board (NTSB) "... concluded that Kennedy experienced a severe case of spatial disorientation while descending over water at night, and consequently lost control of the aircraft. Kennedy did not hold an instrument rating and was therefore only certified to fly under visual flight rules. However, at the time of the accident the weather and ambient light conditions were such that all basic landmarks were obscured, making visual flight challenging, *although still legally permissible.*

"Atmospheric conditions along Kennedy's flight path on the night of the crash were occasionally hazy, which can lead to spatial disorientation for pilots. However, the weather was officially listed as visual meteorological conditions (VMC), which allowed Kennedy to fly under Visual Flight Rules (VFR) rather than Instrument Flight Rules (IFR). However, the visibility was very poor in Essex County, New Jersey, and airports along Kennedy's flight path reported visibilities between five and eight miles with haze and a few clouds. Some pilots flying similar routes as Kennedy on the night of the accident reported no [visible] horizon over water because of haze." Also, the NTSB reported [that] one pilot cancelled a similar flight that evening due to "poor" weather. The [weather] conditions near the crash site were described as clear skies at or below 12,000 feet; visibility 10 miles.

> Better to be on the ground wishing you were flying, than in the air flying, wishing you were on the ground.

Kennedy's accident is not unique. There are more than a few documented cases of well-trained medical evacuation helicopter pilots who have succumbed to the weather, especially at night. I have popped a time or two into the clouds myself at night. Gratefully, the clouds were nothing more than little puffs of visible moisture, nothing widespread, not enough for me to become solid IFR. Weather reporting services cannot know everywhere what the cloud conditions are like. Unfortunately, often at night, a cloud is not visible until you are in it.

I apologize for using Kennedy's unfortunate accident to begin this dialogue. But it highlights a very important first principal about flying *anywhere*. And does so without regard to any specific set of rules, whether VFR or IFR. How a pilot is to control his aircraft, however, should certainly dictate the rules he is to follow.

VMC vs IMC

THE ACRONYM VMC (visual meteorological conditions), mentioned in Kennedy's accident report, is defined in the FAR/AIM as: "Meteorological conditions expressed in terms of visibility, distance from cloud, and ceiling equal to or better than *specified minima.*"

The FAR/AIM goes further to define VFR conditions as: "Weather conditions equal to or better than *the minimum for flight under visual flight rules.*" Specified minima obviously mean the minimums as spelled out in FAR Part 91.155 "Basic VFR weather minimums," where the table stipulates for each class of airspace and defined altitude the required cloud clearance and minimum visibility standard the VFR pilot must abide by to be legal (and I might add, safe).

It appears that the two definitions are nearly identical. The former states "equal to or better than specified minima" while the latter states "equal to or better than the minimum for flight under visual flight rules." *Specified minima*, therefore, seems to also mean the *minimum for flight under visual flight rules*.

In the same vein, the acronym IMC (instrument meteorological conditions) per the FAR/AIM is defined as: "Meteorological conditions expressed in terms of visibility, distance from cloud, and ceiling *less than the minima* specified for visual meteorological conditions."

The FAR/AIM further defines IFR conditions as: "Weather conditions *below the minimum* for flight under visual flight rules."

In this case, too, the former definition appears the same as the latter.

I find these definitions misleading.

To correct this deficiency, I would like first to say that the weather, how it appears and how it is reported, will dictate the flight rules that *may* be followed or that are *required* to be followed. There can be no question about this. Furthermore, the weather also determines how the aircraft is to be controlled: either by visual reference to the natural horizon or the ground, or by the sole use of the flight instruments.

Let's return to Kennedy's unfortunate accident. The FAR/AIM does not define or give reference to *inadvertent* IMC, which is unintended flight into such *atmospheric* conditions whereby visual reference to the ground is lost, the very conditions Kennedy must have encountered. At some point during his flight, Kennedy turned away from the coastline directly toward Martha's Vineyard. He was now over open water with apparently no visible horizon and no ground reference lights. He may have been "legal" with respect to cloud clearances, and ground stations along the coastline may have reported visibilities better than the minimum for VFR flight, but once he lost all visual references, he needed above all else (purely for longevity) to rely solely on his flight instruments to control the aircraft. This is where I introduce the obvious and I hope logical notion that …

… if the pilot can control his aircraft without the need of his flight instruments, he is effectively in VMC (visual meteorological conditions) despite the FAR/AIM definition. If he must rely solely on his flight instruments to control the aircraft, then he is in IMC (instrument meteorological conditions) regardless the FAR/AIM definition. (Even if an autopilot is used, it does not negate the prevailing atmospheric conditions.)

In neither case does this new definition regard the *reported* weather nor does it account for VFR [weather] conditions versus IFR [weather] conditions. With Kennedy's situation, he was legal to fly under visual flight rules. However, by having no means to control the aircraft visually once over open water, he was in instrument meteorological conditions (IMC) which required him to revert to the onboard flight instruments for aircraft control (and to follow instrument flight rules and procedures). (However, a pilot not trained or versed in IFR procedures would be hard pressed to suddenly know how to handle an instrument approach procedure in an emergency.)

If flight in visual weather or visual [atmospheric] conditions implies the pilot has visual reference to the natural horizon or the ground, then Kennedy had neither. If flight in instrument [atmospheric] conditions implies flight in such conditions whereby the pilot has neither visual reference to the natural horizon nor the ground, then the pilot must use his flight instruments to control the aircraft. In the broadest sense, instrument flight is flight based solely on the use of the flight instruments to control the aircraft. In the broadest sense, then, visual flight is flight where the instruments *are not needed* to control the aircraft.

The above discussion is singular in focus, and just happens to reiterate that first fundamental principle: how the aircraft is to be controlled—by visual means or by sole use of the aircraft flight instruments.

Aircraft Control

AIRCRAFT CONTROL. What is it? How is it defined? It depends, I say, on what you want the aircraft to do. If you want straight and level flight, the evidence is a steady heading in the direction you want to go, and the altitude and airspeed you want to maintain. If the values chosen are apparent on the instruments—*that* is aircraft control. If you choose not to use your flight instruments as evidence, or if they are not visible, then if you are in decent visual conditions, the aircraft is under control if the aircraft is not turning wildly and there is no exaggerated nose high or nose low attitude. More bluntly—if you aren't scaring the crap out of yourself. If your control panel and instrument lights go out during a night flight, can you find your way to the airport, and can you activate the runway lights, and can you land without a landing light? If you can do all that the aircraft is under control—so long as you can somehow see the earth or the horizon, even in relative darkness. In instrument conditions, with no visible *anything* outside the cockpit, the artificial horizon (attitude indicator) is your key instrument. All the rest are trend instruments. The VSI (vertical speed indicator) informs you that you are in a climb or descent; the altimeter notifies you that it happened. The turn and bank instrument indicates you're turning; the directional gyro informs you that it happened. Keeping the ball centered tells you the aircraft is *slipping* through the air rather than *slamming* through it. The yaw instrument is the least understood and perhaps the most vital, to preclude spatial disorientation. During unusual attitude recovery practice, think wings level, trim, pitch, and power. Repeat it over and over until the aircraft is straight and level: wings level, trim, pitch, and power. Repeat. Repeat.

What are your cockpit priorities? On a long and boring flight, if you are wanting something to do, do this:

1. Is the aircraft under control?
2. Do I know where I am?
3. Do I understand my last communication (clearance, instructions) with ATC?
4. Are my engine performance instruments reading in the green range?
5. How's the weather out there? Icing? Are there thunderstorms up ahead?
6. Fuel—is there enough? Why not do a fuel check.

The first three items are your *primary* priorities. The next three are your *secondary* priorities. Obviously, if the aircraft is not under control, get it under control — your first priority. If you aren't sure where you are exactly — get found. If ATC has your mind muddled — get it unmuddled. If one of your engine gauges is flickering, think forced landing. If a tornado is veering your way — backtrack, fast. And if your fuel gauge is galloping toward zero ... what can I say? Was the gas cap fastened correctly? Who knows?

Whenever my students couldn't decide what they should be doing, I had them do all the above. What else is there to do? A pilot's job is never ending.

Aircraft control is more than making sure you aren't upside down. It's ensuring that your assigned heading, airspeed, and altitude are as required. During radar vectors, ATC issues clearances and instructions based on each pilot doing his best precision flying. Orientation: if radar malfunctions woe be the pilot who hasn't kept track of his progress in the airspace to give an accurate position report. You must quiz ATC any instructions not completely understood. No blundering through the airspace. A pilot must listen to his aircraft for telltale signs of a failure. A pilot must use all his senses: hearing, smelling, feeling, even taste. An odd smell should raise an eyebrow. An unfamiliar vibration can spell disaster (especially in a helicopter). When the flavor in the back of your mouth goes sour, something in your gut is warning you that something is rotten in Denmark.

I've had a couple of female flight nurses claim they were psychic. One day on our way to Poplar Bluff from Springfield, Missouri, one of them made this statement: "I have a bad feeling about this flight." The gooseflesh rose over my body. The day was perfectly clear, not a shred of anything to be concerned about. I asked what she meant, thinking we were about to fall out of the sky any minute, any second. "Oh, I just think we're going to have a problem with the patient." We got to Poplar Bluff, we loaded the patient, who was going for a heart transplant, we made it back to Springfield — nary a sniffle of a problem. Aircraft *and* patient did just fine. I take premonitions seriously. The ones that emerge from deep in the gut are a caution from *somewhere*. There is always the possibility that something can go haywire on any flight. To me, a psychic warning is a reminder that though "flying is not inherently dangerous, it can, however, be very unforgiving of human error." I become ever more vigilant, ever more cautious. I have come within two miles of landing at a scene at night when I aborted. On the way, I detected the signs of fog — not too blatant but obvious enough to know that fog could be an issue on the way back to the hospital with the patient onboard. I was right. Fog did become an issue but not before landing at the hospital emptyhanded. We humans are not limited to our five senses; we do have a sixth sense, the sense that sees into the future, maybe not in full detail but enough to raise our cockles — and spur our curiosity.

Basic "Visual" Flight Rules

A T THE very least, as previously discussed, to fly VFR one must be able to control the aircraft by visual means. Instruments NOT critical nor needed. This also implies enough visibility to LOOK, SEE, and AVOID. *All pilots, regardless the rules, when in visual conditions, must periodically view the skies around them to see obstructions or other aircraft in time to avoid a collision hazard.* One must steer clear of clouds, certainly. If the visibility is low, the VFR pilot must go slow enough (without allowing the aircraft to stall) to see an obstruction or other aircraft in time to avoid a collision.

Reflecting on Kennedy's unfortunate accident, had there been a quarter moon or better, and perhaps the dimmest demarcation between heaven and earth (the surface of the ocean), he might have made it to Martha's Vineyard unscathed. Spatial disorientation is an insidious "physiological-mental" condition. Once it takes hold the inevitability of disaster is almost certain. I recall one day during my basic instrument training the "feeling" of going up and backwards. It was midafternoon. Sunlight was pouring through the rotor system of the TH-13T "instrument training

helicopter" from behind, causing a rapid flickering on the instrument panel. By the time my flight instructor took control, I had the helicopter in a sixty-degree nosedive. My belief in the instruments was non-existent, thus I countered the feelings I had (the seat of my pants) with forward cyclic (control stick) and a complete reduction of power (the collective lever full down).

Bell Helicopter TH-13T

More than likely Kennedy simply became overwhelmed by the loss of all visual references. I can well imagine his mind racing like a rat caught in a maze, his inexperience as a pilot unable to settle himself long enough to think clearly, to focus on aircraft control, and to call ATC for assistance, to be guided by radar toward the nearest airport claiming full visual conditions. His wife and sister-in-law were probably no help at all. (We army pilots called this OBE, over become by events.)

My last flying position as an EMS "flight for life" helicopter pilot was in the Rio Grande valley. In February 2008, a fatal accident occurred due to unforeseen atmospheric conditions. The crew (nurse, paramedic, and pilot) were reacting to a medical emergency on South Padre Island. It was at night. At about one thousand feet the pilot supposedly encountered a layer of clouds over the lagoon that separates the Island from the mainland. Once the dispatcher learned he had lost radio contact with the crew, a search ensued. Rescuers found the helicopter nose down in the lagoon, in four feet of water. With all visual references lost, the pilot obviously succumbed to vertigo, and thus failed to maintain control of the aircraft. Luckily, they hadn't yet picked up the patient, otherwise there might have been four fatalities instead of three. It behooves any pilot to understand any and all ramifications of spatial disorientation, how it might come about, how to counter it. And particularly how to avoid it.

Per the FAR/AIM, basic VFR describes the minimum cloud clearance and visibility standard for "visual" flight in the different classes of airspace, which we will discuss in detail later.

Clear of clouds is a given. Some amount of forward visibility is also a given. For example, low-level scud running (dodging clouds at low altitude) is often a  disaster in the making. Whereas a helicopter pilot can slow his aircraft to a mere crawl, an airplane pilot must have enough forward visibility to compensate for the speed of his aircraft. The higher the stall speed (the greater the forward speed), which means the greater the forward visibility needed. A helicopter pilot can land at most any open space should he encounter lowering visibilities. An airplane pilot needs a minimum required length of runway or open and level area upon which to land. Low-level scud running at night is too ridiculous to contemplate, much less discuss. There is no merit to this kind of activity. However, because army pilots are trained to use night vision goggles (NVGs), leave it to the U.S. Army to require pilots, for the sake of combat effectiveness, to fly in such conditions.

VFR Conditions vs IFR Conditions

FOR THE sake of legalities, flight is conducted either in VFR conditions or IFR conditions. As defined in the Introduction, VFR [weather] conditions are those *meteorological conditions equal to or better than the minimum for flight under visual flight rules.* Conversely, IFR [weather] conditions are those *meteorological conditions below the minimum for flight under visual flight rules.* Simply put, if the class of airspace within which you are conducting a VFR flight requires that you maintain a certain distance from clouds, anything less than the distance required automatically implies flight in IFR [weather] conditions. If the minimum visibility requirement is three statute miles, should the inflight visibility fall below that value, flight is now being conducted in IFR [weather] conditions. It doesn't matter that you might have visual contact with the ground (to control the aircraft). Any inflight visibility less than that required quite literally means that following visual flight rules is no longer an option. Thus, instrument flight rules and procedures must be applied.

At what point during his VFR flight did John F. Kennedy, Jr. become quasi-illegal? He was supposedly nowhere near a cloud, the reported visibility at ground stations generally along his route of flight was greater than that required for VFR flight, yet he presumably had no visual contact with either the ground (the surface of the ocean) or the natural horizon, due to the dark of night coupled with the atmospheric condition of haze. He quite literally had zero visibility to guide by (to control the aircraft). If you happen to punch into a cloud on a VFR flight, losing all visual references, how is this any different than Kennedy's situation? There is no difference. Kennedy was, by the strict definition, *legal* but he and his passengers consequently became *legally dead*.

If this so-called legal mumbo-jumbo confuses you, please remember that if you cannot control the aircraft by visual means, it means you must revert to your flight instruments. If you must do this you cannot at the same time look out, see, and avoid. Besides, what can you see through an opaque windshield? Nothing. The whole idea behind the rules that apply to both visual flight and instrument flight are based on the principle of avoiding a collision hazard with — *anything*.

On occasion ATC (air traffic control) will ask a pilot his flight [weather] conditions. A VFR pilot who states anything less than VFR conditions could find himself in deep doodoo. If he knows he is closer to any cloud than is allowed, he best relocate himself at the appropriate distance away. An IFR pilot who is in the clouds may declare IFR [weather] conditions: certainly true. Better still to announce he is solid IFR (IMC) — in such conditions where he cannot see anything outside the cockpit. This tells the controller that should any potential target become visible on his radar screen, the chance of the pilot seeing it is nil.

One other aspect of basic VFR has to do with the cloud ceiling over a given airport. If an airport is within designated controlled airspace such as Class B, C, D, or surface Class E, when the ceiling is less than 1,000 feet and/or the visibility is less than 3 statute miles the airport is considered IFR. A special clearance to operate VFR is then required. More on this later.

All in all, minimum cloud clearance and visibility requirements enhance the notion of safety for all pilots, VFR and IFR alike.

Let's now examine VFR cloud clearances. There is the bare bottom minimum of **clear of clouds**. This is anywhere anytime, day or night, in a helicopter or an airplane. Instrument rules and procedures imply flight in or near a cloud — or in zero visibility conditions. Visual flight rules imply the ability to see outside the cockpit to both control the aircraft and to see and avoid a collision hazard.

Typically, the **standard cloud clearance** is 500 feet below, 1,000 feet above, and 2,000 feet horizontal along with a 3-statute mile minimum visibility. The **expanded cloud clearance** is 1,000 feet below, 1,000 feet above, and a 1-statute mile horizontal distance with a 5-statute mile minimum visibility. *(From here on I will not state the "above and belows," I will refer to bottom line basic VFR as: clear of clouds, standard basic VFR, or expanded basic VFR, and their associated minimum visibilities.)*

Why these values?

Since IFR pilots are permitted to be in a cloud or close to one, as they fly along descending, climbing, entering cloud after cloud, the last thing an IFR pilot needs to see is a VFR aircraft closer to a cloud than the regulation allows. The space or distance the VFR pilot is required to be from any and all clouds allows both the VFR and IFR pilot time to see and avoid each other. If you as a VFR pilot are barely beneath a cloud (still able to see the ground to control the aircraft), don't be surprised if an IFR pilot on descent out of that same cloud smashes right into you. Or if you as a VFR pilot are directly above a cloud, skimming the tops, don't be surprised if an IFR aircraft climbs directly into your belly. Horizontal distances allow both the IFR and VFR pilot time to react as they approach head-on, or should their paths be destined to cross perpendicularly.

Again, anytime a VFR pilot is closer to any cloud than the regulation allows, that pilot is technically in IFR [weather] conditions. Anytime the flight visibility is less than allowed for the VFR pilot, he is technically in IFR [weather] conditions. It might be difficult to judge distances from clouds during the day, so give them a wide berth. It is far more difficult at night.

Basic "Instrument" Flight Rules

INSTRUMENT FLIGHT rules are remarkably simple. First, you must be instrument rated. This entails going through the training to become IFR qualified. Second, you must be instrument current, meaning you must have conducted recent instrument proficiency per the regulation. Third, your aircraft must be certified for flight in IFR [weather] conditions. If flight is to be conducted in controlled airspace, you must file an IFR flight plan and have received an appropriate air traffic control IFR clearance. If IFR flight is to be conducted in uncontrolled airspace, the regulation also stipulates, apart from receiving an ATC clearance, that you must choose an appropriate altitude along your route of flight to clear obstacles by a given amount. Also, per your magnetic course, you must choose the appropriate odd/even cruising altitude. These are the basic rules. The odd/even rule is designed, I believe, to keep you from colliding with other IFR aircraft flying in the same area. (See FAR 91.179 paragraph [b] IFR cruising altitude or flight level **in uncontrolled airspace**.)

Since this book is about explaining both visual and instrument flight rules, where instrument flight becomes tricky or difficult is dealing with the procedures: departure procedures, enroute procedures, arrival procedures, and instrument approach procedures. Same-same with VFR flight. The tricky part is understanding the requirements for visual flight operations in the different classes of airspace.

Restrictions to Visibility

A SIDE FROM remaining clear of clouds, forward and surrounding visibility are vitally important. Let us list the several defined restrictions to visibility per the FAR/AIM. The most notable is fog, which is nothing more than a ground-hugging cloud. Then there is rain and drizzle and snow, mist and haze and smoke, blowing sand, dust, and volcanic ash—the list goes on. Anytime the visibility is less than the optimum that can be reported, there will be some reason for the limitation such as these just mentioned. The report might also say that the rain, freezing rain or snow pellets, are light, moderate or heavy. You can have light rain and freezing fog, widespread mist and haze, heavy rain showers, thickening smoke from forest fires. What you see through the cockpit windshield that doesn't look good, probably isn't good. If an airport has weather-reporting capability and the visibility is clear all around, then the visibility is likely to be reported at about seven or ten miles, even though once in the air you can see forever in all directions (e.g., out west in Arizona or Colorado).

To explain further, let's assume that the best visibility that can be reported at an airport is seven miles. If the visibility is less than seven miles the report must stipulate why, what is causing the visibility to be less than maximum? Is it fog, light rain, smoke, haze, mist? This then gets us into the minimum VFR visibilities allowed in the different classes of airspace. Since five statute miles is the "max" minimum and three miles or 1 mile or 1/2 mile is the lowest, some atmospheric phenomena is causing these low values. What is causing the visibility to be 5 statute miles, for example? Seven statute miles and more is considered good VFR visibility. It cannot be overemphasized the importance of good flight visibility. Nor can it be overstated what reported factors limit visibility, because each factor has its own peculiarities. Fog, for example, over time, comes and goes, lifts and descends, expands and contracts. Haze on the other hand tends to be rather uniform over a given area, also over an extended length of time. I saw this uniformity while operating out of Johnstown, Pennsylvania, during the summer of 1988. Smoke from a forest fire, for example, shifts with the prevailing wind, thick in one direction, dissipating in another, and cannot be considered uniform.

Low visibility coupled with low clouds is rarely uniform over a given area. Thus, if you are inclined to do low-level scud-running, don't be surprised if one day you find yourself boxed in, unable to turn left or right, no place to go, the weather has closed in behind you. (The medical crew always became antsy when the visibility wasn't seemingly clear in all directions. And when they became antsy, I was checking the reports from surrounding airports to reassure them.)

Controlled Airspace

THE NATIONAL airspace has been sliced and divvied and quartered to such a degree that pilots I'm sure believe that they may very well be tip-toeing through a minefield. Gaze at any VFR sectional or low altitude IFR enroute chart to know what I mean, or gander at an instrument approach plate with all its "chicken scratches."

If such a display were made visible into a "hardened actuality" certainly no pilot would venture his aircraft into such a maze of tripwires. The hardened actuality only exists in our minds. As a VFR pilot, should you dare to fly close to a busy terminal area such as Atlanta or Dallas or Los Angeles, you had better know precisely where you are. To collide with a large airliner carrying hundreds of passengers, best you not live through the experience. The FAA will draw and quarter you, a death far more painful than a sudden impact with the ground.

Long before the massive proliferation of aircraft, back when there were no lawyerly-written bureaucratic rules and regulations, pilots had to fend for themselves to keep safe. Common sense ruled. Common sense still rules, however the rules and guidelines are deviously intricate. We just need to ferret out their reasoning, which is the purpose of this book.

Per the FAR/AIM, controlled airspace is that airspace designated as Class A, B, C, D, and E. If the airspace doesn't have one of the above class titles, the airspace is Class G (uncontrolled) airspace. So, airspace is either controlled or uncontrolled and can't be both regardless of any other title an airspace area might have. (To be discussed later.)

The rules governing VFR flight in the national airspace are designed both to keep the VFR pilot from running into other VFR pilots as well as obstacles on the ground, and just as importantly to keep VFR aircraft from interfering with the flight of IFR aircraft. Each of the controlled airspace classes has a hierarchy. Class A airspace is more restrictive than Class B airspace, which is more restrictive than Class C, which is only slightly more restrictive than Class D, which is decidedly more restrictive than surface Class E, which is more restrictive than general Class E, and which is naturally more restrictive than Class G "uncontrolled" airspace. But more restrictive to what? The answer: *To VFR operations.*

Class A Airspace

FORMERLY TITLED Positive Control Area (PCA), this area "… is that airspace from 18,000 feet MSL up to and including Flight Level (FL) 600, including the airspace overlying the waters within 12 nautical miles off the coast of the 48 contiguous States and Alaska; and designated international airspace beyond 12 nautical miles off the coast of the 48 contiguous States and Alaska within areas of domestic radio navigational signal or ATC radar coverage, and within which domestic procedures are applied." (FL 600 somewhat equates to 60,000 feet MSL.)

First, let's explain what "positive control" means. It means that air traffic control has complete jurisdiction to manage the flight of every aircraft within this airspace for the purpose of collision avoidance. Because visual flight rules are *not applicable* within Class A airspace, VFR flight is not permitted, *regardless the weather.* Only those aircraft operating under instrument flight rules and procedures may be in this airspace.

How does ATC exercise positive control of aircraft? ATC does this by issuing clearances. A clearance is ATC authorization, for collision avoidance purposes, to proceed in controlled airspace under specified conditions. The "specified conditions" or elements of a proper clearance (called a route clearance) are:

1. Limit
2. Route of flight
3. Altitude
4. Expectation

These route clearance elements will be discussed further in Part Two, Instrument Flight Procedures Explained. Suffice it to say, when ATC issues a clearance, he does so subject to *known* air traffic, those pilots to whom he has already issued a clearance, or who he is about to issue a clearance. All clearances issued are designed to keep aircraft apart by a standard amount of distance. So long as each pilot follows his clearance to the letter, no aircraft should ever get any closer to any other aircraft than how their respective clearances specify.

What aircraft fly in this vast Class A airspace? Certainly, the airlines, and just as likely corporate and the military. Why no VFR aircraft? Even if the skies were clear forever in every direction, and periodically they are, instrument flight rules predominate because of the requirement that ATC have positive control over all aircraft and the only way to exercise this control is with a route clearance, the tool by which ATC separates aircraft, particularly in instrument weather conditions. *This means that all pilots must be instrument rated.*

During flight in Class A airspace, it is entirely likely, too, that marginal weather conditions will be encountered. Pilots must therefore be skilled in aircraft control using the flight instruments. Regarding instrument flight rules, not only must the pilot be proficient in IFR procedures, his aircraft must be properly equipped and certified. Sound radio procedures are the mainstay of instrument flying (at least in controlled airspace). In controlled airspace, ATC expects all pilots to be experienced enough to follow clearances and other instructions to the letter knowing full well the intent (and implication) of such instructions.

If visual flight is loosely defined as willy-nilly flight, constantly sidestepping clouds by some proper amount, ATC can hardly have the kind of control needed to keep aircraft apart by a prescribed amount if VFR pilots are erratically wandering through the air like bumblebees.

The atmosphere above 18,000 feet MSL is quite rarified. Closure rates between aircraft are extremely fast. Standard separation in Class A airspace is much greater than at lower altitudes. Thus, the airspace most restrictive to VFR flight is Class A airspace by simply not allowing it to occur. *VFR flight is verboten.*

Class B Airspace

BEFORE THE great airspace name change, this airspace was titled Terminal Control Area, or TCA, which I think is a more appropriate label.

Visualize such airport monsters as Denver International (DIA), Chicago O'Hare, Dallas/Fort Worth, Los Angeles International (LAX), New York Kennedy Airport, Atlanta Hartsfield Airport, New York La Guardia, etc. These and a few others are the biggies, those airports with numerous airline traffic, both landing and departing. The FAR/AIM defines Class B airspace as "… that airspace from the surface to 10,000 feet MSL surrounding the nation's busiest airports in terms of IFR operations or passenger enplanements. The configuration of each Class B airspace area is individually tailored (in fact, DIA tops out at 12,000 feet MSL) and consists of a surface area and two or more layers (some Class B airspace areas resemble upside-down wedding cakes), and is designed to contain all published instrument procedures once an aircraft enters the airspace. An ATC clearance is required for all aircraft to operate in the area, and all aircraft that are so cleared receive separation services within the airspace. The cloud clearance requirement for VFR operations is *clear of clouds*." The minimum visibility requirement for VFR operations is *3 statute miles*.

Weatherwise, VFR operations in Class B airspace is not very strict. On the other hand, a VFR route clearance from ATC is classically restrictive: enter Class B airspace at point A and go to point B via such-n-such route at or below some specified altitude, expect something else at point B, etc., all the while remaining clear of clouds and maintaining at least 3 statute miles visibility. Those are tall orders, the very reason access into or through Class B airspace for the VFR pilot is so restrictive. If there is any way the VFR pilot can avoid Class B airspace, he should elect to do so.

Let's face it, a collision between a large airliner carrying numerous passengers and a light, single-passenger VFR aircraft is not an even trade. Like operations in Class A airspace, all aircraft are required to be under positive air traffic control. Since IFR aircraft descending from Class A airspace through Class E airspace into Class B airspace are already under air traffic control, the transition is hardly worthy of comment. All airline pilots departing Class B airspace are required to file IFR, and follow instrument flight rules and procedures, since they will eventually penetrate Class A airspace. (In fact, airline pilots always file IFR, no matter where they depart from or where they are going. That way marginal weather is never a concern.)

A word or two about 3 statute miles visibility. Some weather phenomenon is causing the visibility to be that low: light rain, maybe light snow flurries, fog, mist, haze, a ragged ceiling. If ATC senses that the weather is not likely to remain generally uniform throughout his Class B airspace, he is not likely, either, to allow VFR operations since his top priority is all his IFR air traffic.

Terminal Radar Service Area

IT IS necessary to discuss the TRSA because it is the forerunner of Class C airspace, formerly titled Airport Radar Service Area (ARSA). So many alphabet-soup acronyms; it's mindboggling. Again, with collision avoidance as our theme, and with so many restrictions placed on VFR pilots—so that they won't or can't interfere with IFR operations, particularly those aircraft carrying hundreds of passengers, a little history lesson goes a long way to our understanding of visual flight regulations and the various controlled airspace areas.

In a nutshell, per the FAR/AIM, "… TRSAs were originally established as part of the Terminal Radar Program at selected airports. (I shall name five airports currently serviced by TRSAs to give you an idea of some of their locations: Maxwell AFB, Montgomery, AL; Fairbanks International Airport, Fairbanks, AK; Hector International Airport, Fargo, ND; Capital City Airport, Harrisburg, PA; and Great Falls International Airport, Great Falls, MT.) TRSAs were *never controlled airspace* from a regulatory standpoint because the establishment of TRSAs was never subject to the rulemaking process … Part of the Airport Radar Service Area (ARSA) program was to eventually replace all TRSAs. However, the ARSA requirements became relatively stringent and it was subsequently decided that TRSAs would have to meet ARSA criteria before they could be converted. TRSAs do not fit into any of the U.S. airspace classes; therefore, they will continue to be non-Part 71 airspace areas where participating pilots *can receive additional radar services* which have been redefined as TRSA Service.

"Pilots operating under VFR are *encouraged* to contact the radar approach control and avail themselves of the TRSA services. However, *participation is voluntary* on the part of the pilot.

"TRSAs are depicted on VFR sectional and terminal area charts with a solid black line and altitudes for each segment." (The *Class D portion* is charted with blue segmented lines and a blue airport symbol.)

Okay, let's break this down. Class C airspace is controlled airspace. Prior to the name change, the ARSA was controlled airspace as was the Terminal Control Area, now titled Class B airspace. Class D airspace, yet to be discussed, is controlled airspace and is a *very small* part of a TRSA (though, as mentioned, the TRSA by itself is NOT considered controlled airspace). Clear as mud? Because a TRSA is not controlled airspace, pilots are not required to participate in TRSA services. But are highly encouraged to do so. (As of this writing I count 31 selected airports across the country surrounded by TRSA airspace. Also, as of this writing, I count 90 selected airports surrounded by Class C airspace.) What prompted this proliferation of ARSA (Class C) airspace, this attempt to change all TRSAs into ARSAs?

This is my theory. On Monday, September 25, 1978, per the NTSB official report "… one of this country's worst aviation disasters occurred when Pacific Southwest Airlines (PSA) Flight 182 collided with Cessna Skyhawk N7711G 2,600 feet over the city of San Diego. Instead of landing safely at San Diego International Air-

port as planned, Flight 182 smashed into the streets of the city itself. A total of 144 people died (seven on the ground). In the Cessna, two people died as their light aircraft exploded on impact with the Boeing 727's right wing. Trailing flames and smoke from its wing, still carrying 128 passengers and seven crew, Flight 182 slammed into the ground at 300 mph. All 135 people on board died. Only four of their bodies were found intact. On the ground, first responders were confronted with scenes worthy of the Apocalypse."

At the time of the accident, the airspace surrounding San Diego International Airport was not considered a Terminal Control Area, nor was it enclosed by TRSA airspace, and not by ARSA airspace. It was just an airport into which and out of which commercial airline traffic operated. The day was sunny, the skies were clear, the winds were calm. A perfect day for flying. A day you wouldn't expect a disaster of such monumental proportions. (I learned that the San Diego airport, after doing a VFR sectional recon, is and has been enclosed by Class B airspace.)

I cannot confirm anything I write here, but there is always blowback to an aviation mishap of such magnitude. The result of congressional investigations prompted rule changes. From then on *certain* TRSA airspace became the newly minted ARSA airspace, which finally became by the great name change Class C airspace, whereby VFR participation **became mandatory instead of (just) voluntary.**

Class C Airspace

THIS AIRSPACE, formerly titled Airport Radar Service Area (ARSA), is next in descending order for enhanced restrictions to VFR operations. Per the FAR/AIM, Class C airspace is "… that airspace from the surface to 4,000 feet above the airport elevation (charted in MSL) surrounding those airports that have an operational control tower, are serviced by a radar approach control, and that have a certain number of IFR operations or passenger enplanements ..." all the features of Class B airspace but not as magnanimous as: Miami International Airport, San Francisco International Airport, Boston Logan Airport, etc. To name a few airports surrounded by Class C airspace, they are: Tucson International, Jacksonville International, Indianapolis International, Des Moines International, Reno/Tahoe International, Pope Air Force Base, North Carolina, Austin-Bergstrom International, Texas, Burlington International, Vermont, and Colorado Springs Airport.

"Although the configuration of each Class C airspace area is individually tailored, the airspace usually consists of a 5 nautical mile radius core surface area that extends from the surface up to 4,000 feet above the airport elevation, and a 10 nautical mile radius shelf area that extends no lower than 1,200 feet up to 4,000 feet above the airport elevation." This means that the configuration is a scaled down version of a Class B upside-down wedding cake.

IFR operations within Class C airspace are no different than in Class B airspace or Class A airspace (or for that matter, in any class of controlled airspace). More on this later.

Still, for VFR operations, "... two-way radio communications must be established with the ATC facility providing ATC services prior to entry and thereafter maintain those communications while in Class C airspace." Standard basic VFR applies. These cloud clearance criteria are considerably more restrictive than for VFR flight in Class B airspace. (I don't know why.) *ATC provides permission to enter Class C airspace, but no air traffic control clearance – nor air traffic separation.* ATC simply wants to know who you are, where you are, your altitude, and your intentions. ATC provides radar-generated advisories only. Whereas a full-blown air traffic control clearance is designed to specifically keep aircraft apart by a given amount of space, VFR operators in Class C airspace can fly any which way they please. If, however, ATC offers the VFR pilot a plan of action to avoid another aircraft, he best follow it. Should ATC be overwhelmed with his IFR/passenger plane traffic, permission to enter Class C airspace may be forestalled or negated altogether.

Fortunately, or unfortunately, depending on your perspective, should you as a VFR pilot wish to fly within the boundaries of a TRSA, and wish to avail yourself of ATC radar services for advisories, and should the controller be too busy, he can deny you radar advisory services but he cannot deny you access to the TRSA, *because it is not, by title, controlled airspace* (though it might lie wholly or partially within Class E airspace, its configuration, too, much an upside-down wedding cake). This is quite unlike VFR operations within Class C airspace. If ATC is too busy to talk to you, and so implies or states, this in effect denies you access to Class C airspace.

As we have previously discussed, landing and departing airline traffic around busy airports require an extra measure of safety to keep disasters at bay. Since, as I have already mentioned, IFR air traffic (regardless the weather), is always in communication with ATC (in controlled airspace), for VFR air traffic to be in touch with ATC, *the rules must be modified to require VFR pilots to be so.*

It goes without saying that collision avoidance is greatly enhanced when VFR pilots take advantage of ATC radar services whenever possible. During approach and landing, including departing, airline pilots are hampered by busy cockpit procedures and a limited view out the cockpit, as they search for targets even on a clear day. The pilots of PSA Flight 182 were advised of the Cessna in their vicinity, and may have had visual contact once, but soon lost sight of it in the ground clutter of buildings and houses, thus PSA Flight 182 descended directly on top of the Cessna.

Class D Airspace

NEXT IN descending class hierarchy is Class D airspace. It is identified on VFR sectional charts as a blue airport symbol. Typically surrounding the blue airport symbol are segmented blue circular lines. This airspace is commanded by a tower operator tasked with the orderly flow of both VFR and IFR air traffic. It was formerly titled *Airport Traffic Area*. The segmented blue lines represent the former title of *Control Zone*. (There is no equivalent airspace term for *control zone* in the new nomenclature.)

First, what is the primary function of the tower operator? When does an airport warrant a tower operator? How is a tower operator different than a so-called *bonafide* air traffic controller?

When any airport (in either Class G or surface Class E air-

> The most dangerous part of flying is driving to the airport.

space) over a set period, meets a daily minimum threshold of air traffic, it is time to consider creating a control tower with a tower operator, the person who will manage the upswing in air traffic. His primary duty then, unlike a *bonafide* air traffic controller, is to sequence competing users for takeoff and landing, as well as to arrange aircraft movement on the airport surface, typically on a first come first serve basis, dependent also on location. For example, a pilot in parking calls for permission to taxi to the active runway. Another pilot somewhere else on the airport surface calls next for taxi instructions. Depending on their individual locations the tower operator advises both pilots the actions they are to take to meet their requests. In the meantime, as the pilots proceed to their destinations on the airport surface, each is tasked with visually avoiding each other and any other obstacle in their paths.

If two aircraft call inbound for landing from two different locations, the tower operator coordinates their movements as expeditiously as possible, giving priority to the pilot whose position affords the best opportunity to land first. The operator is likely to advise both to maintain visual separation as they approach the airport. Thus, the pilots are obligated to adjust airspeed and flight path accordingly. Clearance to land is merely permission to plant the aircraft on the runway, assuming the runway is clear of aircraft and/or any obstructions. A clearance to takeoff is merely permission to advance down the runway to become airborne. If there are other aircraft in the traffic pattern the pilot is required to maintain visual separation.

Does IFR air traffic have priority over VFR air traffic? Not necessarily. Regardless the status, landing aircraft have priority over those aircraft on the ground. If an IFR aircraft on an instrument approach has finally broken out of the clouds and is in position to safely land the aircraft, depending on where other aircraft are in the traffic pattern will determine who does what first. A VFR aircraft turning on final approach may be allowed to land ahead of the IFR aircraft if there is enough separation between them. In other words, in visual conditions all aircraft are required (by regulation) to look, see, and avoid each other. Whoever is given priority over others, as dictated by the tower operator, "the others" are required to give way.

As previously mentioned, air traffic control (ATC) issues clearances designed to keep aircraft apart by a given amount of space. He does this by telling the pilots which route to fly, how high to fly, where their route is intended to take them. A tower controller does none of this. He merely *sequences* aircraft. It is up to the pilots to maintain their own separation however they see fit. Aircraft movement in the vicinity of an airport primarily assumes visual conditions. Air traffic control of enroute aircraft between airports assumes nonexistent visual conditions.

Per the FAR/AIM, Class D airspace "extends upward from the surface to 2,500 feet above the airport elevation (charted in MSL) surrounding those airports that have an operational control tower ... Two-way radio communication must be established with the ATC facility providing ATC services prior to entry and thereafter maintain those communications while in Class D airspace." This is like VFR aircraft operations in Class C airspace. The tower operator, in this case, needs to know who is in his airspace so that he can advise the pilot and/or sequence other pilots accordingly. VFR weather criteria to operate is the same as for VFR operations in Class C airspace: standard basic VFR.

Surface Class E Airspace

THIS IS one aspect of Class E airspace that must be discussed ahead of general Class E airspace (and the control zone concept listed below).

Surface Class E airspace is denoted by magenta segmented lines, either circular or rectangular, generally around or in the vicinity of any airport that has a preponderance of IFR traffic. Surface Class E airports have not met the criteria warranting a control tower, but they do warrant, due to a certain volume of IFR operations, the legal means to limit VFR air traffic when the ceiling and visibility are reported to be less than 1,000 feet and/or less than 3 statute miles, respectively. Special VFR permission (by ATC) is then required to operate within the airspace below that ceiling. When the ceiling and visibility do not require any kind of VFR restriction (other than to maintain standard basic VFR), the airspace is open ended. VFR pilots can come and go at will. No radio communication is required except to make courtesy announcements to other pilots in the vicinity, on the common traffic advisory frequency (CTAF).

> Flying is not inherently dangerous, but can be very unforgiving of human error.

The Control Zone Concept

PER THE FAR/AIM, when an airport that is surrounded by one of the following classes of airspace: Class B, C, D, and surface Class E, reports weather to be ceiling less than 1,000 feet and/or visibility less than 3 statute miles, there can be no VFR operations within the airspace unless cleared by ATC. This clearance when requested by the VFR pilot is titled Special VFR.

The reason for limiting the activities of VFR operations during these marginal weather (IFR) conditions is so that said VFR aircraft will not and cannot interfere with landing and departing IFR air traffic. A special VFR clearance then is designed to steer VFR pilots away from IFR air traffic.

Again, how do you recognize *surface* Class E airspace? On VFR sectional charts, those airports surrounded by segmented magenta lines signifies such surface Class E airspace. The airport symbol itself will likely be magenta-colored as well. As previously discussed, those airports with an operating control tower will be recognized with a blue airport symbol and will be titled Class D airspace. Surrounding the blue airport symbol are typically segmented blue lines signifying a level of IFR air traffic greater than normal into or out of that airport. There is no need to color-code Class C or Class B airspace this way; it is automatically understood that there is a preponderance of landing and departing IFR air traffic in these areas. Which begs the question: when does an airport warrant surface Class E airspace classification? The answer: when a minimum threshold of IFR air traffic activity is reached. This is the same as "when does an airport warrant an operating control tower and control tower operator?" The answer: when a minimum threshold of both VFR and IFR air traffic activity surrounding that airport is reached.

We see then that collision avoidance is enhanced when such operating rules are put in place. Air traffic control isn't simply for the sake of satisfying big brother. Anytime you can prevent an air disaster such as the one that occurred in the San Diego area between a small VFR aircraft and a large passenger airliner is a good thing.

How do you request and then receive a special VFR clearance? Within surface Class E airspace, a request may be made through a flight service station. In Class D airspace the request should be made through the tower operator. In Class C and B airspace, the request is made through clearance delivery. (Clearance delivery is nothing more than a separate frequency upon which to receive a clearance, to reduce radio frequency congestion on other frequencies more used for other vital purposes.) Each special VFR request is passed on to the air traffic controller in charge of the airspace in question. Since he knows where his IFR traffic is located, what clearances he has issued, he is the one who issues the S-VFR clearance to steer the VFR pilot away from that traffic.

A special VFR clearance to *depart* an airport might come to a VFR pilot like this: "ATC clears Cessna 1234 out of controlled airspace to the south (or north or east), at or below 500 feet. Maintain special VFR. Report clear of controlled airspace."

A special VFR clearance to *enter* controlled airspace for landing: "ATC clears Cessna 1234 into controlled airspace from the north (or east or south), at or below 500 feet. Maintain special VFR. Report airport in sight." Or words to that effect. What does it mean? "Maintain special VFR." For helicopters it means remain clear of clouds. For fixed-wing traffic it means remain clear of clouds and have a 1 statute mile visibility during daylight (3 statute miles at night). No minimum visibility for helicopters. Depending on the airport, other minimum criteria might apply. (One last word regarding special VFR, whether required in Class D airspace or surface Class E airspace. Aside from the fact that those airports have a certain number of IFR operations, implying at least one instrument approach procedure for use by the IFR pilot, I have also studied these airports and have surmised that some level of scheduled airline service also prevails, small commuter airplanes that fly to and from major hub airports, maybe not in every case, and maybe not many commuter operations, mind you, but enough to warrant the need of a special VFR clearance during marginal weather.)

General Class E Airspace

AS I read the FAR/AIM, general Class E airspace is that airspace that is controlled, but is not classed as A, B, C, D or surface Class E. Prior to the great FAA name change, general Class E airspace was separately titled *Transition Area*, *Control Area* and *Continental Control Area*.

Transition Areas are easy to spot. Look at any VFR sectional chart and note all those airports that appear surrounded by magenta-colored, inward-shaded areas, typically circular or keyhole configured, but can be any shape needed to define the dimensions of the transition area. The map legend states that the base of these areas begins at 700 feet AGL. Outside of these "transition areas," the base of Class E airspace begins at some other value as noted. Why this sharp downward push of controlled airspace over these selected airports? As previously mentioned, I have done research on this and am 99% convinced that anytime you see these magenta-shaded circles or keyholes, there is at least one (maybe more) published instrument procedure(s) for use at that airport. Below 700 feet AGL is uncontrolled airspace *where basic VFR is clear of clouds*. Outside the magenta-shaded circles or keyhole configurations, controlled airspace generally begins at 1,200 feet AGL. So, the so-called transition area push-down is creating an added buffer of controlled airspace requiring VFR pilots to steer clear of clouds by standard basic VFR criteria. Why? To better protect IFR pilots during descent on an instrument approach. That's really it in a nutshell. Hopefully, when the IFR pilot descends below 700 feet AGL he should be in visual conditions able to see the runway and land. Below 700 feet AGL, a VFR pilot must merely remain clear of clouds and have some amount of visibility to operate VFR, at least one half to one to three statute miles. Adequate, I suppose, to preclude colliding with the instrument-rated pilot just prior to his landing.

The definition of the formerly-titled **Control Area** airspace was that area intended to protect the Victor airway system, as these airways crisscrossed the national airspace. Generally, this airspace began at or above 1,200 feet AGL. (Below 1,200 feet AGL was uncontrolled airspace.) East of the Rockies, this airspace was everywhere above 1,200 feet AGL. Over the Rockies and westward, the Victor airways were protected by control area corridors. Think standard VFR cloud clearances and minimum visibility values to expanded cloud clearances.

Lastly, was the **Continental Control Area** designation of controlled airspace, or "everywhere else controlled airspace" which extended above 1,500 feet AGL regardless the MSL to 18,000 feet MSL, the base of Class A airspace (formerly the PCA). For all Class E airspace, there are two basic VFR levels: from the surface up to but not including 10,000 feet MSL for which standard basic VFR applies. At or above 10,000 feet MSL, expanded basic VFR applies. (Class E airspace also extends beyond Class A airspace to infinity. I believe this is to signal to the world that all airspace over the United States is inviolate. To invade our airspace with nuclear-tipped missiles is to invite a reciprocal response.)

Class G "Uncontrolled" Airspace

PER THE FAR/AIM, uncontrolled airspace is any airspace not classed as A, B, C, D, or E. Thus, it has the designation of Class G airspace. Class G airspace practically blankets the entire country from the surface to the overlying controlled airspace. It is entirely possible to fly coast to coast, border to border, and never leave uncontrolled airspace (i.e., enter controlled airspace). To know how to do this a pilot must reference all applicable VFR sectional charts.

Generally, if a pilot remains below either 700 feet AGL or 1,200 feet AGL, depending, and if he avoids penetrating the boundaries of Class B, C, D, and surface Class E airspace (mostly those airspace areas surrounding airports of notable merit), the chance of entering controlled airspace is virtually nil.

VFR flight in uncontrolled (Class G) airspace is complex as per the FAR/AIM. For the purpose of defining basic VFR, Class G airspace is broken into three layers:

1. at or below 1,200 feet AGL regardless of MSL;
2. more than 1,200 feet AGL but less than 10,000 feet MSL; and
3. more than 1,200 feet above the surface and at or above 10,000 feet MSL.

The first layer addresses basic VFR weather minimums for flight in a helicopter and an airplane, during the day and at night. Because a helicopter is so much more maneuverable, and can be slowed to a walking hover, the weather minimums are almost non-existent. Clear of clouds and basically go slow enough to see an obstruction or other aircraft in time to take evasive action. The minimum visibility for a helicopter is 1/2 statute mile for day and 1 statute mile for flying at night. An airplane pilot must have during daylight a 1-statute mile minimum visibility and a 3-statute mile minimum visibility for night. Before the FARs changed, all a helicopter pilot needed day or night was to remain clear of clouds—no minimum visibility was required. This almost meant (in effect) that a helicopter pilot could fly in reported zero-zero conditions (certainly not the intent of the powers that be).

If you find yourself in the second layer: more than 1,200 feet AGL but less than 10,000 feet MSL, whether in a helicopter or an airplane, during the day you need 1 statute mile visibility along with standard basic VFR cloud clearances. At night all pilots need 3 statute miles visibility and cloud clearances remain the same. (I don't know how you can see well enough at night to maintain proper cloud clearances, much less see a cloud. To top that, three statute miles minimum visibility at night is not enough to see anything, especially a cloud, according to my learned experience. Besides, what weather phenomena is causing the visibility to be that low?)

One reason for cloud clearances at all in the second (and third) layer is that it is permissible to fly IFR in uncontrolled airspace, typically conducted at no less than 1,000 feet above the ground and certainly higher.

Finally, above 1,200 feet AGL and at or above 10,000 feet MSL, all aircraft, day or night, need 5 statute miles minimum visibility and 1,000 feet below, 1,000 feet above, and 1 statute mile horizontal cloud clearances (those previously defined as *expanded* cloud clearances).

A little more about Class G "uncontrolled" airspace. It is airspace where ATC has no authority to control and separate aircraft. In other words, within this airspace ATC has no "legal" jurisdiction to manage the flight of any aircraft. It is VFR and IFR free-for-all airspace, even though certain FAA minimum weather criteria apply (for VFR aircraft), as stipulated above. IFR aircraft, of course, are not required to remain clear of clouds by any margin, or have any minimum visibility. Their restrictions have to do with altitude: to always be high enough to clear any obstruction (tower, mountaintop, etc.) by a given height, that is along their route of flight; and to abide by the odd/even altitude rule to avoid a collision with other IFR aircraft flying in the same area.

I once made the comparison between an airplane and a helicopter, based on their aerodynamic characteristics. An airplane is something you *go somewhere in* and a helicopter is something you *do something with*. The "doing something with" is now my focus thus explaining how convenient it is to operate a helicopter in "uncontrolled" Class G airspace without an air traffic controller dictating or knowing your every move.

The maneuverability of a helicopter allows a helicopter operator to perform any number of useful tasks (at or below 1,200 feet AGL regardless the MSL) such as logging, seismic exploration, game count, power pole line construction, power line inspection and maintenance, stocking rivers, lakes and ponds, "flight for life" operations in remote locations, search and rescue, radio tower construction, helicopter skiing (positioning skiers on top of a ski slope for their downhill run), heli-lifting stranded wild animals to safer locales, I'm sure the list could go on.

Thus, another reason basic VFR weather criterion in Class G airspace are so liberal. Logging pilots can skirt low-lying clouds in their operational area. One half mile visibility during the day isn't much, but pilots do have pilot-in-command authority to cease activities as they see fit. As with any VFR operation (in VMC) pilots are required by regulation to LOOK, SEE, and AVOID obstacles and nearby aircraft.

VFR Flying vs IFR Flying

IF TO fly VFR is to maintain constant visual contact with the ground or the natural horizon, or in essence be able to control the aircraft without the need for the flight instruments, and at the same time keep a proper distance from clouds and have the minimum flight visibility, then it appears that a VFR pilot's access to the national airspace is basically limited by the weather, by cloud coverage, and those atmospheric conditions that hamper visibility.

If to fly IFR in the national airspace is to not have the least concern for VFR limitations regarding the weather (aside from thunderstorms and icing conditions), then one can see that an IFR pilot has nearly unlimited access to the national airspace.

But what is the real difference between the two sets of rules? One major difference is that IFR flying is precision flying, whereas VFR flying may be willy-nilly flying limited only by the weather. Not only must an IFR pilot be able to control his aircraft precisely by his flight instruments (in instrument meteorological conditions), he must maintain prescribed altitudes to clear obstructions by a given amount, thus he must navigate precisely the exact centerline of his desired course. If IFR flight is conducted in controlled airspace, then radio contact with, and clearances given by, air traffic control is an absolute must. Thus, "precise" radio communications with ATC is also an absolute necessity.

It is entirely possible to fly VFR coast to coast, border to border, and not be required to communicate with anyone, a similar declaration I made earlier about flying VFR across the United States not ever leaving uncontrolled Class G airspace (that is, entering controlled airspace). In fact, with the weather at its minimum worst of 1/2 statute mile to 1 statute mile visibility, while remaining clear of clouds during daylight hours, you might not even be limited by the weather. Again, flying in such weather is akin to scud-running, not all that good in a helicopter and certainly worse in an airplane. So, VFR flying is not precision flying nor is it flight that necessarily requires communication with ATC. Even if the weather is clear from top to bottom and everywhere in between, VFR flight does not have to represent strict government control. If the weather is not a factor, VFR pilots do have considerable access to the national airspace.

Is it permissible to fly IFR in "all-around" clear weather? Certainly, it is done all the time. But why bother, if following visual rules is so much easier and/or simpler?

Several reasons:

1. Following instrument rules, especially in controlled airspace, is a sure-fire way of having constant flight following protection (for search and rescue purposes).
2. Under the strict control of ATC, every IFR pilot is afforded standard separation between all *known* IFR aircraft, plus VFR traffic advisories in a radar environment.
3. Should the pilot following IFR in VFR [weather] conditions suddenly encounter IFR [weather] conditions, he doesn't need to steer clear of such conditions since he is already operating on an IFR flight plan.

In other words, if you have an instrument rating, why not use it even in great weather. The best way to gain proficiency dealing with ATC, receiving and understanding clearances, is to do it when weather isn't a factor, so that if you get confused you can always cancel your IFR status and proceed VFR.

Instrument flying isn't all about keeping the aircraft under control by referencing your flight instruments; it's also about communicating with ATC, receiving clearances, understanding the implications of your clearance, then following through with the intent of the clearance. (To be further discussed in Part Two.)

Special Use Airspace

THE UNITED States government has lots of toys and they like to play with them in the national airspace. Guns, missiles, rocket firing, exploding land-based artillery shells; and a few areas they need to keep under wraps, you know, top secret; plus, areas where government officials gather to make merry (silly legislation and behind the scenes radical decisions). Per the FAR/AIM, "... special use airspace consists of that airspace wherein activities must be contained because of their nature, or wherein limitations are imposed upon aircraft operations that are not a part of those activities, or both. Except for controlled firing areas (CFAs), special use airspace areas are depicted on aeronautical charts …"

The best way to describe special use airspace is that the areas have defined dimensions, effective times, and some level of danger to the unwary public.

Whatever the government is doing inside the area had better not exceed the boundaries of the area. There are to be no rockets or missiles that land outside the airspace on top of a town, or farm house, or major highway. At the same time, due to these dangers, you best not wander into the airspace if you ain't got no business being there. Only participating aircraft are allowed in the area, probably because they are the ones making all the noise, creating all the danger.

By strict definition, special use airspace is NOT *controlled airspace*. Special use airspace, however, may lie wholly within, wholly outside or partially within one of the classes of controlled airspace, mainly general Class E airspace. It is highly unlikely that any portion of special use airspace would lie within areas surrounding busy airports, particularly if rockets are launched and machineguns are fired. *(Basic VFR applies to that portion of special use airspace that lies within the boundaries of any of the classes of airspace, controlled or uncontrolled.)*

There are two distinctions that need to be made in our understanding of special use airspace. First, participating versus non-participating aircraft. Second, using agency and controlling agency. The controlling agency is generally DoD, or the Department of Defense. The using agency is typically one of the arms of the DoD, such as the Army, the Navy, the Air Force, or the energy department, or any governmental body needing the *special use* of certain airspace areas. (The using agency may also be ATC, when the DoD users are done playing with their toys.)

Participating aircraft are those aircraft permitted to be in special use airspace, meaning they are probably the ones creating the danger, and if not, by design, they have permission to be there, such as Marine 1 helicopter picking up the President on the White House lawn. Non-participating aircraft are not allowed, unless permission is requested from and granted by the controlling and/or using agency. So, let us examine special use airspace, their dangers and restrictions.

Prohibited Areas and National Security Areas

PER THE FAR/AIM, prohibited areas "… contain airspace of defined dimensions identified by an area on the surface of the earth within which the flight of [non-participating] aircraft is prohibited. Such areas are established for security or other reasons associated with the national welfare." Three very notable buildings: The White House, the U.S. Capitol, and the Supreme Court are protected by prohibited area airspace. Even Mt. Vernon, George Washington's former home, is protected (P-73). In fact, there is a giant flight "restricted" zone around all of Washington, D.C. Any aircraft not scheduled, or not following the strict path into Ronald Reagan National Airport, for example, is first given a warning. If the pilot doesn't show any sort of compliance immediately, he'll be taken down by one of the countless surface-to-air missiles located around the capital.

Similarly, national security areas "… consist of airspace of defined vertical and lateral dimensions established at locations where there is a requirement for increased security and safety of ground facilities. Flight through NSAs is not prohibited and no special advance clearance or authorization need be obtained to enter them. However, pilots of aircraft *are strongly encouraged* to either stay clear of NSAs or obtain prior authorization to pass through them in order to reassure the controlling agency that no threat to national security exists. NSAs are a compromise between normal airspace and restricted or prohibited airspace. NSAs can be temporarily converted into restricted airspace by NOTAMs (notice to airmen). On VFR sectional charts, NSAs are delimited by a heavy dashed magenta border and a special notation." For example, east of Pueblo, Colorado, is the Pueblo Chemical Depot, protected by a national security area. Should a plane happen to crash land inside the depot's confines toxic chemicals might be released.

So, although these two defined special use airspace areas, by description, do not have any kind of unusual hazardous activities going on within their boundaries, the hazardous activity of a surface-to-air missile can flat ruin an unsuspecting pilot's day. *Nonprohibited* flight over an NSA may still prompt a trigger-happy security person to shoot first and ask questions later.

Restricted Areas and Warning Areas

LIKE THE two previously discussed special use airspace areas, warning areas and restricted areas are also similar. They contain activities within their boundaries that are hazardous to non-participating aircraft. Per the FAR/AIM, "… restricted areas contain airspace identified by an area on the surface of the earth within which the flight of aircraft, *while not wholly prohibited*, is subject to restrictions. Activities within these areas must be confined because of their nature or limitations imposed upon aircraft that are not a part of those activities, or both. Restricted areas denote the existence of unusual, often invisible, hazards to aircraft such as artillery firing, aerial gunnery, or guided missiles. Penetration of restricted areas without authorization from the using or controlling agency may be extremely hazardous to the aircraft and its occupants."

"A warning area is airspace of defined dimensions, extending from three nautical miles outward from the coast of the U.S., that contains activity that may be hazardous to non-participating aircraft. The purpose of such warning areas is to warn non-participating pilots of the potential danger. A warning area may be located over domestic or international waters, or both." The same kind of aerial gunnery, guided-missile firing, shooting, etc., performed by the United States Navy (over open water) is not one bit different than U.S. artillerymen firing their cannons from the outskirts of the main post of an army base such as Fort Hood, Texas, or Fort Carson, Colorado. The U.S. Air Force at Hurlburt Field near Eglin AFB in Florida uses a restricted area (over land) to fire machineguns from a C-130 aircraft (typically at night). When I was based at Destin, Florida, as an EMS helicopter pilot, many times I radioed the Air Force and asked them to shut down the C-130 firing so that I could expedite my way to the hospital in Pensacola to deliver a patient. They were always happy to oblige.

Not all activity within a restricted area has artillery going off, or guns shooting, or missiles firing. All along our southern border with Mexico there are high-altitude balloons tethered to steel cables that extend to 15,000 feet MSL. One is located just south of Fort Huachuca, Arizona (R-2312); another is located SSW of Deming, New Mexico (R-5115); and another is located right on the border southwest of Carrizo Springs, Texas (R-6316); and still another (R-6317) is north of Rio Grande City, Texas. To wander through these circular-configured restricted areas is to invite a steel cable slice through the wing. The diameter of these areas is about 10 nautical miles. Due to winds aloft, I would gather that these balloons create a significant arcing of the cable as they are attached to the ground.

Alert Areas and Military Operations Areas

THESE TWO areas are also similar and yet different. "Alert areas are depicted on aeronautical charts to inform non-participating pilots of areas that may contain a high volume of pilot training or an unusual type of aerial activity. Pilots should be particularly alert when flying in these areas. All activity within an alert area must be conducted *in accordance with CFRs, without waiver*, and pilots of participating aircraft as well as pilots transiting the area must be *equally responsible for collision avoidance.*"

By contrast, "MOAs consist of airspace of defined vertical and lateral limits established for the purpose of separating certain military training activities from [civilian or otherwise] IFR traffic. Whenever a MOA is being used, non-participating IFR traffic may be cleared through a MOA *if IFR separation can be provided by ATC.* Otherwise, ATC will reroute or restrict non-participating IFR traffic."

"Examples of activities conducted in MOAs include, but are not limited to: air combat tactics, air intercepts, aerobatics, formation training, and low-altitude tactics. Military pilots flying in an active MOA are exempted from the provisions of 14 CFR Section 91.303 (c) and (d) which prohibits aerobatic flight within Class D and Class E surface areas, and within Federal airways." I can't see how the military might desire to perform aerobatic flight within the surface areas of Class D and E airspace, unless an airshow is in progress. But aerobatic flight within Federal airways means this manner of flying could be performed most anywhere in general Class E airspace. From somewhere near the ground to the beginning of Class A airspace at 18,000 feet MSL, military flight "shenanigans" are certainly likely to interfere with all IFR traffic, civilian or otherwise. (Since Class A airspace caters to only IFR aircraft, and most of the flights are typically high-capacity passenger jetliners, it is unlikely that any special use airspace inhabits this area. Airline schedules cannot be interrupted or delayed, and the activities of military pilots in a MOA would certainly not enhance safety among airline pilots and passengers.)

It therefore goes without saying that "... Pilots operating under VFR should exercise extreme caution while flying within a MOA when military activity is being conducted."

I would like to think that the difference between these two areas is clear. In an alert area all aircraft are equal, civilian and military, VFR and IFR, regarding proper flight operations. While I was at Fort Rucker, I recall all the various training activities within the alert area: low-level navigation, day and night transition training at the various stage fields, instrument training—there were probably 250 helicopters in the air at once. On the other hand, highspeed fighter jets within a MOA may perform any number of maneuvers in and out of the clouds. Only if you are performing a civilian (or otherwise) IFR flight might you be rerouted if a MOA is active, if ATC can't keep you separated from the wild antics of military aircraft, even if the weather is clear.

Controlled Firing Areas

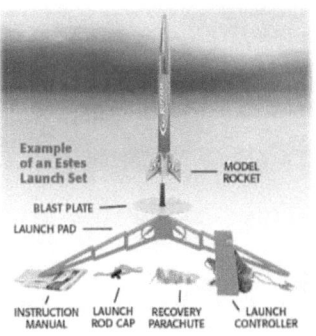

Example
of an Estes
Launch Set

BLAST PLATE —
LAUNCH PAD —

MODEL
ROCKET

INSTRUCTION   LAUNCH   RECOVERY   LAUNCH
MANUAL   ROD CAP   PARACHUTE   CONTROLLER

LASTLY, "CFAs contain activities which, if not conducted in a controlled environment, could be hazardous to non-participating aircraft. The distinguishing feature of the CFA, as compared to other special use airspace, is the activities are suspended immediately when spotter aircraft, radar, or ground lookout positions indicate an aircraft might be approaching the area. There is no need to chart CFAs since they do not cause a non-participating aircraft to change its flight path."

West of Pueblo, Colorado, on Highway 50, near Cañon City, is a model rocket company: *Estes Industries*. Though I have never witnessed any model rocket launches, I can well imagine that this location could be a prime example of a controlled firing area. Other examples of activities within CFAs are: ordnance disposal, blasting, static testing of large rocket motors, and police and/or public shooting ranges, etc.

Other Airspace Areas

MILITARY TRAINING routes (MTRs), Temporary Flight Restriction (areas), Parachute Jump Aircraft Operations, Ultra-light, Paragliding, and Glider Flight areas, all can pose restrictions or dangers to unsuspecting, non-participating pilots. On VFR sectional charts parachute and hang-glider symbols denote such locations. A TFR area can be so designated during special events or during a natural disaster: such as the New Year's Day Rose Bowl parade or a wildfire or an earthquake, respectively. There is a no-fly zone over Disney World in Florida. All such locations must be either charted (if relatively permanent), or posted through NO-TAMs. The national airspace is a very busy place. Special rules even exist for flight over national parks like the Grand Canyon. Pilots should exercise caution when flying over wildlife refuges, so as not to disturb the wildlife and/or experience a catastrophic bird strike. Even though the skies over DIA are not black with airline traffic, every Class B airspace area is or can be a target-rich environment for a VFR pilot bent on suicide. Electronic news gathering (ENG) helicopter pilots compete for exclusive footage of anything newsworthy, often to their own detriment, particularly when two helicopters collide. And the pilots typically don't have enough flight experience to fit in a pill bottle. TFAs often restrict ENG activities to preclude such a disaster. Special Air Traffic Rules and Special Flight Rules Area(s) exist where VFR aircraft are required to communicate with ATC. One such area is the Eglin AFB/Valparaiso community complex. (As mentioned, San Diego has the benefit of Class B airspace, though it isn't listed in the FAR/AIM.)

Conclusion

IN THE order of presentation, VMC vs IMC has precisely to do with pilot aircraft control, by outside visual references or reliance on the instruments. VFR conditions vs IFR conditions, the legal aspect of visual flight rules. VFR vs IFR, the rules and procedures governing flight in the national airspace. The differing classes of airspace: controlled vs uncontrolled, and their hierarchy. Special use airspace: their operating restrictions and the dangers inherent in each.

I have shown that the hierarchy of controlled airspace restricts or limits VFR operations progressively. Within Class G "uncontrolled" airspace, VFR flight operations are limited regarding airplane versus helicopter, day versus night, and altitude. IFR pilots experience no such change in flight operations from one class of controlled airspace to another.

The purpose of instrument flight rules and procedures is to allow the IFR pilot to fly closer to the clouds than would otherwise be permitted. These same procedures may be used in clear weather. Collision avoidance, at least between IFR aircraft, is dramatically enhanced in doing so.

During my VFR solo ferry-flight episodes, I had complete latitude to deviate and wander as the weather dictated. Heavy rain clouds ahead made me alter my course dramatically west of Lexington, Kentucky. Strong headwinds caused me to cut my flight short of my intended destination after departing Lafayette, Indiana (heading for Shreveport, Louisiana). Fog near Quincy, Illinois, caused me to request a special VFR clearance into the Quincy airport. The visibility had reduced to almost a quarter-mile. I remained on the ground for two days before continuing onward to Pennsylvania. In fact, on my trip from Provo, Utah, to West Chester, Pennsylvania, fog hampered my progress from just west of Topeka, Kansas, until after I got to Morgantown, West Virginia. During my time as an EMS helicopter pilot, weather was a constant factor in my GO-NOGO decision-making process. A patient was always better off going by ground ambulance than stuck in the middle of a cornfield because I had to abort due to bad weather. In fourteen years flying EMS, I had to cut my flight short with a patient onboard six times. To me, that was six times too many.

The pilot in command is the final authority
as to the safe and efficient operation of the aircraft.

Part Two

Instrument Flight Procedures Explained

"UH-1 Huey Helicopter"

Introduction

A PROCEDURE is like a recipe. It is a step-by-step way to get something done, like baking a cake. Or cooking a turkey. Or putting together some child's toy, like a bicycle or playhouse. Instrument flying is also a step-by-step process — to get from point A to point B safely, in no less than IFR [weather] conditions.

Each instrument flight procedure is designed to keep the pilot apart from obstructions and other IFR air traffic. IFR flying is ten percent aircraft control and ninety percent thinking ahead of the aircraft. Instrument flying is listening and talking. It is reading and understanding the hieroglyphics that define a procedure. It is being calm, cool and collected midst apparent chaos. It is questioning ATC that which is not understood. It is maintaining instrument proficiency at all levels. It is continuously studying the current FAR/AIM.

Instrument flying doesn't have to be complicated. It depends on how it is studied. If it is studied in a step-by-step manner, concepts can fall neatly into place. If I present the material in this book the way I want, instrument flight should become something to look forward to.

So, let's get started.

Air Traffic Control

A TC's PRIMARY responsibility is air traffic separation, particularly IFR aircraft conducting flight in controlled airspace. Not all controllers have radar as a means of aircraft separation. Radar coverage over a given area may not be complete, as in mountainous terrain or below a certain altitude. Radar can malfunction.

Air Traffic Control Training Facility

Before there was radar, controllers depended entirely on pilot position reports and an estimate to the next *compulsory* reporting point. I point this out to emphasize how important it is to keep track of one's progress on an aeronautical chart. And, thus, to be prepared to function when radar *malfunctions*.

ATC operates on many discrete frequencies. We've discussed the true purpose and function of a tower operator at a tower-controlled airport. He observes the movement of aircraft on the airport surface and in the surrounding airspace. He manages the flow of traffic as they operate in VFR conditions. He sequences airplanes and even the movement of helicopters. The regulation requires that helicopter pilots avoid the flow of fixed-wing aircraft in and around an airport (most likely due to rotor downwash). At a tower-controlled airport, within Class D airspace, for example, two or three discrete frequencies are in play. There is tower frequency, ground control frequency, and sometimes a separate clearance delivery frequency. Depending on the number of flight operations around a busy airport will determine the number of air traffic control personnel needed and thus the number of discrete frequencies required to handle the traffic. Once a frequency becomes saturated, the need for another controller and another discrete frequency becomes paramount, along with a new division of airspace (a new airspace sector). You know a frequency is congested when the controller must speak non-stop to deliver clearances and instructions. This means that the number of aircraft the controller can recall and manage at once has reached a critical threshold.

An approach/departure control facility surrounds all Class B and Class C airspace. Again, depending on the number of aircraft operations will determine the number of controllers and discrete frequencies required to effectively manage air traffic. A "not so busy" approach/departure control facility might have just two sectors: a north & south sector or an east & west sector. The big airports: DIA, Dallas-Fort Worth, Atlanta, etc., might have four or five sectors. As you approach one of these airports you might talk to two or three different sector controllers before you get lined up on final approach. Not all Class C airspace areas operate fulltime. When traffic tapers off a Class C airport might go dormant for the night, then become functional in the morning when airline pilots start their daily runs. The Harlingen Class C airspace is like that, down near Brownsville, Texas. (Even Class D and surface Class E airspace might have effective times as noted on the appropriate VFR sectional chart.)

Then you have ARTCCs, air route traffic control centers, the controllers that hand you off one after the other until you are told to contact approach control at your destination. To travel IFR coast to coast, border to border, requires a long line of communications. You will talk to many air traffic controllers who will tell you how to get through their sectors based on known traffic. No such thing as centralized "government" control over your flight. There are many controlling agents, all with your vital interests at heart, to help you complete your flight.

Radio Communications

PER THE FAR/AIM, "… The single, most important thought in pilot-controller communications is understanding."

Therefore, I say this: it is the pilot's responsibility to study the aeronautical information manual (AIM) as if one's life depends on it—because it does. It is the controller's responsibility to know exactly what he means by what he says to the pilot. It is the pilot's responsibility to question the controller any aspect of what was said that he doesn't understand. Pilots should be VERY curious; controllers should be VERY clear. A pilot should not advance one quarter-mile farther with even a single doubt.

All clearances and instructions must be read back verbatim, followed by the aircraft call sign. ATC must know the right aircraft got the intended message. Don't abbreviate your call sign unless the controller does it first.

Before you talk for the first time on a new frequency, pause long enough to ensure you are not interrupting a radio transmission between ATC and another pilot. If the moment you key your mic, you hear someone else key their mic, release your mic key immediately. No transmission gets through if two mics are keyed at once.

When it came time for my students to talk, I told them I'd rather they never talk *than talk first*. Think before you talk; make certain your message is intelligible. Know what you want to say.

Before I learned this little trick, this is how I was when given instructions by ATC: "Roger, this is Army 1234, turn ... what direction did you say to turn? And climb to what altitude?"

Better this way: "Roger, turn left heading one eight zero. Climb and maintain 4,000. This is Army 1234." I found that when I stated my call sign first, I would immediately forget what the controller told me to do.

There will certainly be a time or two when you have no idea what the controller meant by what he said. It might even be that the controller didn't mean at all what he said. By repeating back exactly what he said, should (hopefully) cause the controller to realize his mistake. If the controller clears you to do something that you *should* know perfectly well what he means, but your brain has shut down, it doesn't hurt to ask for clarification. But you can't do this all the time. You must know *something* without your brain misfiring after every other transmission. That's why your current FAR/AIM is your bread-and-butter publication.

ATC issues clearances and instructions based on what YOU want to do. Do you know where you want to go, how you want to get there? If you don't, how do you expect ATC to help you. Per the AIM, "... Brevity is important, and contacts should be kept as brief as possible, but controllers must know what you want to do before they can properly carry out their control duties. And you, the pilot, must know exactly what the controller wants you to do. Since concise phraseology might not always be adequate, use whatever words are necessary to get your message across." (I call it talking baby talk.)

Whatever the controller tells you to do, you must either agree with it or request an alternate course of action. The controller is not in charge of your aircraft, your life, your wants and needs. You are. The controller is a facilitator. He knows NOT your aircraft limitations, your limitations, your weather conditions, your desires. He's not your boss. He's a person who must consider your request in light of the request of many other pilots. He does his best to juggle the desires of all competing users in the same airspace.

The ATC Clearance

A CLEARANCE issued by ATC is "predicated on known traffic and known physical airport conditions. An ATC clearance means an authorization by ATC, for the purpose of preventing [a] collision between known aircraft, for an aircraft to proceed under specified conditions within controlled airspace.

"It is not authorization for a pilot to deviate from any rule, regulation, or minimum altitude nor to conduct unsafe operation of the aircraft."

Known air traffic versus unknown air traffic. If a pilot and his aircraft are required by regulation to be known to ATC, *he had better be known*. A previous example of this was when we discussed Class C airspace rules for VFR aircraft. Prior to entry into Class C (and Class D) airspace, the VFR pilot is required to call ATC and announce his desire to be in that airspace. Once contact is made, the VFR pilot and his aircraft are now *known*. Prior to contact, the VFR aircraft was *not known*. Known means known to ATC for the purpose of issuing clearances to other aircraft based on the *now known location* of any previously *unknown aircraft*. Say what?

On a bright and sunny day, with VFR pilots out there in droves, it's likely that there is no requirement for VFR pilots to be known to ATC, particularly in general Class E airspace. When ATC issues a clearance to one of his IFR pilots, he does so subject to the location of, and previous clearances issued to, his other known IFR pilots. Those VFR pilots out there enjoying the day and the great weather, are flitting here and there as they see fit. Their only responsibility is to steer clear of any clouds by the required amount, and to look, see, and avoid other aircraft (both VFR and IFR) and/or any obstacles (towers, mountaintops, etc.).

Specified conditions. What are those? Well, if an actual separation between aircraft requires *a certain amount of space between them,* and because aircraft move constantly through the air, there must be some method by which separation is achieved. Route of flight is one. Altitude another. A point in space to go to and no farther is still another. Even speed adjustment is one.

We now get to what constitutes a proper route clearance, their elements and implications:

1. **Clearance limit** — longitudinal separation, a point in space to go to but not go beyond without a further clearance. I call it "separation by time." The clearance limit is an implied stopping point until ATC can resolve traffic conflicts beyond that point. As a pilot approaches his clearance limit, he should automatically think holding. Holding allows ATC *the added time* he needs to resolve traffic conflicts. In the same vein, ATC could just as easily tell the pilot to reduce his speed by some amount. Still, even a speed reduction might not be enough, so holding at the limit is an organized way of stopping. (A clearance limit is also known as a *holding fix*.)

2. **Route of flight** — lateral separation. Separate routes far enough apart are separation by some amount of distance, such as three miles, maybe five miles in Class A airspace. The route of flight could be going direct somewhere; or via some Victor airway; or by a radar vector (heading); or by way of a magnetic course to a non-directional beacon; or by way of a VOR radial to a VOR. Or it could be some combination thereof. The route of flight could even be "as filed" as entered on the IFR flight plan form.

3. **Altitude** — vertical separation. One thousand feet typically, maybe two thousand feet in Class A airspace. Once at Fort Rucker I was one of six helicopters holding over the same radio beacon, one thousand feet apart. I was at nine thousand feet, high enough to get a nose bleed. I'm afraid of heights. What if a transmission light comes on? It's a long way down wondering if the rotor system is going to fail. Anyway, limit, route, altitude, the means by which to be separate from other aircraft.

4. **Expectation** – what does ATC have in store for you at the clearance limit — new routing? a change in altitude? approach clearance? a new clearance limit? Maybe holding instructions. If it is something other than what is implied, it must be verbally stated. Pilots are not mind readers.

Clearance limit. A point in space. A fix with a name that can be identified on an aeronautical chart. It can be as generalized as simply an airport name; or as specific as an intersection on a Victor airway; or a GPS waypoint; or a VOR or NDB NAVAID. Any point in space that can be identified by a pilot's navigation equipment. ATC must know what equipment you have, to know where and how to clear you. If your ADF (automatic direction finder) receiver is inoperative, he can hardly clear you to a non-directional beacon (NDB). Thus, if he clears you to one, you need to remind the controller of your lack of such capability. Then he amends your clearance to reflect what you can do. A clearance limit is not only over a transmitter on the ground, for example, but your assigned altitude makes the limit a true *three-dimensional point in space*.

As you approach your clearance limit, ATC is working to clear you beyond it, to keep you moving along. If he needs you to stop at the limit, he will issue you holding instructions and an expect-further-clearance (EFC) time. If you get antsy, like maybe he's forgotten you, call the controller and tell him you are approaching the limit. If he's busy on the radio talking to other pilots, you must think going into holding on the course you arrive at the limit, standard "righthand" turns. If a holding pattern is depicted on the chart, hold as depicted. Then call ATC and ask for further clearance. Remember, you are not to go any *farther* toward your destination without a *further* clearance.

Route of flight. There are so many ways ATC can clear you to the limit. By radar vectors; by a Victor airway; by a direct course to a NAVAID; by a specific course to a NAVAID; or by a combination of the above. ATC can clear you all the way to your destination (limit) by way of your flight plan route: "… cleared as filed." If the route of flight issued is rather convoluted, and you couldn't write it down verbatim, ask for a repeat, and for the controller to slow down. He doesn't want you stumbling around in the airspace any more than you do.

Altitude. The assigned altitude may or may not be to your liking. Your route of flight might not be to your liking, either. A newly assigned route and altitude may lead you right into towering cumulus where I guarantee you will get your ass kicked. What looks like white puffy innocuous beings pack a punch. Ask the controller permission to go around the cloud buildup. If you are already in the clouds and are in icing conditions, ask for a more favorable altitude. If turbulence is turning your stomach, request a lower or higher altitude. Whatever ATC has told you to do is not set in stone. It can be altered. You ARE the pilot in command.

Expectation. Whenever ATC can inform you of what he has planned for you at or beyond the clearance limit, he should do so. Not only as a courtesy, but it may be a requirement. To receive holding instructions and no *expect-further-clearance* time is improper. You must know when you are to leave holding in the event of two-way radio failure. If he wishes that you prepare for the preferred instrument approach at the destination, he should so state it as an expectation. "… expect the ILS runway two seven approach to Tallahassee." If a written procedure spells out a specific course of action, but the controller wants you to do something different, he should so state: "In the event of a missed approach … fly runway heading to three thousand feet, expect vectors to the Allen VOR," instead of, for example, the published missed approach procedure. Whenever ATC wants you to do other than what is implied (by being written somewhere), he must so state. Again, pilots are not mind readers. An issued clearance by way of a published route has many implications. An alteration to any written procedure must be verbalized by ATC. Much can be said about *stated* versus *implied* — volumes, in fact.

The IFR Flight Plan

IT ALL begins with the IFR flight plan. Where do you want to go? How do you want to get there? When do you want to leave? How high do you want to fly?

Think lost communications. When all else fails, your flight plan route will be the way to go to your destination in the event of two-way radio failure. In other words, if you can't receive any further clearances from ATC, how you filed your route is the final fallback route to follow. So, make it simple.

The altitude you pick may not be the altitude you are cleared to fly, but close. It will probably be the altitude you can expect in a further clearance. So, choose that altitude wisely.

Your actual departure time versus your planned liftoff time will also be a factor. So, make a note of when you leave. You'll be passing that departure time off to FSS (flight service), who will activate your IFR flight plan for search and rescue purposes.

Once your flight plan has been filed, it takes time for ATC to process it and prepare a clearance. Your initial IFR clearance is the one that gets you off and running. It may be amended, however, any number of times as you proceed enroute. Here is an example of an initial clearance:

"ATC clears Army 1234 to the Tallahassee airport as filed. Climb and maintain 3,000. Expect one zero thousand ten minutes after departure. Contact departure on 123.5. Squawk code 6342. Clearance void if not off by 1150 Zulu. Time now 1107 Zulu."

There are several ways you can receive your initial ATC clearance. It depends on the airport you are departing from and how many services (ATC frequencies) it has.

To receive an initial clearance at an airport in Class G (uncontrolled) airspace is probably more involved than receiving one within Class D, C, or B airspace. But let's go from bottom to top. (In fact, it could be even less involved.)

Assume you are at some podunk airport in Class G airspace. You would typically file your flight plan through a flight service station (FSS) by telephone. Or by radio if you can talk and receive through a remote communications outlet (RCO).

The above issued clearance implies departure from a remote airport. Let's break it down. Where is your clearance limit? It's all the way to your destination, the Tallahassee airport. The route of flight is "as filed." The initial altitude is 3,000 feet (MSL) to *expect* 10,000 feet (your requested altitude) ten minutes after departure. Then you are given your initial ATC contact frequency of 123.5 VHF. Your transponder squawk code is 6342. And then a "clearance void" time followed by the current time.

A clearance void time means that if you are not off and reporting to ATC at or before the void time, your clearance as issued is no longer valid. ATC did his juggling based on you being in the system at a certain time. If you report after the void time, ATC must rejuggle clearances as issued to other aircraft. Probably. Or amend your initial clearance. In other words, your path to your destination is based on you getting off the ground no later than 1150 Zulu (GMT). You can't dilly-dally. (Typically, a void time is issued when departing from a remote location.)

Had you been at an airport in Class D airspace, you might have received your initial clearance from the tower, either on ground control frequency or the tower frequency. If within Class C or B airspace, then from "clearance delivery" on the clearance delivery frequency.

Should your radios go on the blink directly after you contact the controller (within ten minutes after departure), then lost communication procedures go into effect. They go into effect no matter when your radios fail.

Two-way Radio Failure

EVERY CLEARANCE issued must consider the big what if ... *what if the radios fail?*

First, what is two-way radio failure? If you, the pilot, can hear ATC talk to you—*you don't have lost communications*, so long as you can let him know you are receiving his transmissions. If you can't hear the controller talk to you, even though he can hear you, *you do have a bonafide case of lost communications*. Second, if ATC (with radar capability) can't hear you respond to his radio transmissions, he can ask you to do something like turn left or right, or press the IDENT button on your transponder, to let him know you can hear him. Third, in a nonradar environment, even if you can hear ATC talk to you, but you have no way of letting him know you heard him, *you have radio failure*. A true case of lost communications can be quite unnerving.

The procedures for handling lost communications on the part of the pilot is this: "... if failure occurs in VFR conditions, or if VFR conditions are encountered after the failure, each pilot shall continue the flight under VFR and land as soon as practicable." After landing call ATC to let him know you are safely on the ground. (This might all be moot with the proliferation of cell phone coverage. Let's assume no cell phone.)

If the failure occurs in IFR conditions,

Route of flight: (in the proper order)

1. "By the route assigned in the *last* ATC clearance received;
2. "If being radar vectored, by the *direct route* from the point of radio failure to the fix, route, or airway specified in the vector clearance;
3. "In the absence of an assigned route, by the route that ATC has advised may be *expected* in a further clearance; or
4. "In the absence of an assigned route or a route that ATC has advised in a further clearance, *by the route filed in the flight plan.*"

Altitude: at the highest of the following altitudes or flight levels for the route segment being flown. (All published route segments have an MEA—minimum enroute altitude. However, if not on a published route segment, you might be hard-pressed to know the exact minimum altitude to be at. For example, ATC knows minimum vectoring altitudes, something the pilot is not likely to know. But the pilot can ask.)

1. "The altitude or flight level assigned in the *last* ATC clearance received;
2. "The minimum altitude (converted, if appropriate, to minimum flight level as prescribed in §91.121(c) for IFR operations (this having to do with pressure altitude setting of 29.92, for example, in Class A airspace); or
3. "The altitude or flight level ATC has advised may be *expected* in a further clearance."

Leave clearance limit: (also incorporates when to leave enroute altitude)

1. "When the clearance limit is a fix from which an approach begins [at the destination airport], commence descent or descent and approach as close as possible to the *expect-further-clearance* [EFC] time if one has been received, or if one has not been received, as close as possible to the estimated time of arrival as calculated from the filed or amended (with ATC) estimated time enroute [ETA].

2. "If the clearance limit is not a fix from which an approach begins [this assumes a clearance limit short of the destination airport], leave the clearance limit at the *expect-further-clearance* [EFC] time if one has been received, or if none has been received, upon arrival over the clearance limit, and proceed to a fix from which an approach begins and commence descent or descent and approach as close as possible to the estimated time of arrival [ETA] as calculated from the filed or amended (with ATC) estimated time enroute [ETE]." (A little mental gymnastics in higher math.)

All the above as per the FAR/AIM. I think it can be correctly assumed that if ATC has a lost commo aircraft on his hands, he will do everything possible to keep all air traffic away from *wherever the troubled aircraft is likely to go based on the verbatim lost communication procedures.* In a radar environment it is probably a simple matter of watching the radar scope to see where the pilot is going and to then vector other aircraft out of the way. In a nonradar environment, ATC might clear the path ahead on the airway to include clearing all initial approach fixes of all possible approaches at the destination airport. The pilot can also transmit *in the blind* to whomever is listening (hopefully ATC), and announce his intentions. Radio failure is an emergency in IFR conditions. And in an emergency all pilots are allowed by regulation to take whatever steps necessary to ensure a favorable outcome, including breaking every rule in the book.

Introducing lost communications now implies that I have an ulterior motive, and I do. As we proceed onward in our understanding of IFR procedures, as mentioned, every communication with ATC must entail the notion of two-way radio failure. What if … I receive holding instructions, but no expect-further-clearance time? What if ATC issues me a new (amended) clearance that takes me off my flight plan route, and no expect further routing? What if ATC issues me a vector heading without explaining the purpose for the vector? In other words, what if ATC has a mental lapse and doesn't do his job? It's up to the pilot to make sure all bases are covered, since it's the pilot who is in the air, by far more vulnerable than ATC, who is fat and happy in his comfortable chair with a hot mug of coffee to warm his mitts.

Departure and Arrival Procedures

FROM AN airport in Class G (uncontrolled) airspace, your initial clearance might come like this: "ATC clears Cessna 1234 to the Grand Junction airport as filed. *Join Victor 484 prior to ICORY intersection* (these are your departure instructions). Climb and maintain one four thousand, expect one seven thousand ten minutes after departure. Contact Denver Center 125.35 on climb out. Squawk 4576.

Clearance void if not off by 1309 Zulu. Time now 1214 Zulu." Assume you are departing from the Monte Vista Municipal airport about ten nautical miles north by northwest of Alamosa, Colorado.

First, Victor 484 is the filed flight plan route to Grand Junction. After liftoff, the controller is asking you to intercept that route prior to reaching ICORY intersection on that airway. (ICORY intersection is 17 nm due north of the Monte Vista airport.) Nothing complicated about this. From whichever runway you depart, aim as soon as you can toward V-484 to join the airway prior to ICORY. There are no written departure procedures to follow, just ATC instructions. This may be the case in most all departures from remote locations, or from airports within surface Class E or D airspace.

If departure is from an airport in surface Class E airspace, there may not be written departure procedures, either. Just air traffic control instructions that are specific to your aircraft, or to the time of day, and/or dependent on other aircraft wishing to depart at about the same time. As previously mentioned, I have conducted a little research and have found this to be truer than not. Most airports within surface Class E airspace have scheduled "commuter" airline service, usually during daylight hours. A commuter airplane shuttles passengers from remote locations to hub airports like Denver or Salt Lake City, etc., and from DIA or Salt Lake City to remote locations. Surface Class E airspace is added protection from the random wanderings of VFR aircraft when the weather is marginal. (Refer back to Part One *The Control Zone Concept.*)

Departure from a tower-controlled airport in Class D airspace may be simple (as within surface Class E airspace), or there may be a written, coded, departure procedure (SID) that applies. As an example, from the Eagle County Regional Airport in Eagle, Colorado, an airport in Class D airspace, there are two SIDs (standard instrument departure procedures), one (Meeker Three Departure) that aims northwest toward Meeker, Colorado, and another (Gypsum Six Departure) that heads northeast toward Kremmling, Colorado. These two SIDs use VOR NAVAIDS. A third departure procedure (Bevvr One Departure) is defined by RNAV (area navigation), or GPS. From the route description and the direction, I gather that the Bevvr One Departure gets you into the Denver International Airport Class B airspace area. The other two merely get you on your way and beyond.

Because Eagle, Colorado, is surrounded by mountainous terrain, these published departure procedures not only simplify delivery of a clearance, they probably help the pilot avoid obstructions.

These three written departure procedures are complex. For ATC to relay to the pilot every nuance of any one of them would take considerable time on the radio. Again, a procedure, as described in the Introduction (Part Two), is a step-by-step way to get something done. To clear a pilot via the Meeker Three Departure or Gypsum Six Departure or Bevvr One Departure is to say a lot in a very short span of time. The pilot, to receive and comply with such a clearance(s), must have a copy of the procedure with him in the cockpit.

To depart from airports within Class B or C airspace, there may be numerous departure procedures, leading in every possible direction. From DIA, I count twenty SIDs (standard instrument departure procedures). The BAYLR FOUR DEPARTURE from Denver, for example, describes a procedure for departing from each of the eight runways. There are two transitions associated with the BAYLR FOUR DEPARTURE. In addition to its complexity, there are minimum altitudes to maintain, along with an associated distance for each route segment. ATC uses SIDs to reduce his "talking on the radio" workload.

A STAR, standard arrival route, is a SID *in reverse*. However, an arriving aircraft, coming into Denver, for example, may approach from any one of several directions, and for each direction there is a published arrival procedure. (I counted 24 STARs leading into DIA.) As previously mentioned, a STAR like a SID, reduces controller workload, simplifies clearance delivery procedures, and enhances safety by also reducing radio frequency congestion.

As mentioned, instrument procedures per se are a methodical process in written format designed to enhance the flow of air traffic. An IFR procedure has many parts, each part a route segment with an associated course, distance, and some type of altitude restriction or requirement.

Enroute Procedures

THERE ARE dozens and dozens of Victor airways that crisscross the United States, just like the Interstate or major four-lane highways. For example, Victor "airway" 100 (V-100) begins at, by my map recon, the Litchfield VOR 111.2 (LFD) in Michigan, west of Detroit, and simply meanders westward 1,012 nautical miles until it ends at the Medicine Bow VOR 111.6 (MVW) in Wyoming, north by northwest of Laramie. For example, I wish to fly to Laramie, Wyoming, from the Hillsdale airport south and east of the Litchfield VOR. I am given the following ATC clearance: "ATC clears Cessna 1234 to the Laramie (WY) airport direct Litchfield VOR, then via Victor 100. Climb and maintain 3,000. Expect 7,000 ten minutes after departure. Contact Cleveland Center on 120.45. Squawk 3464. Clearance void if not airborne by 1200 Zulu. Time now 1110 Zulu."

What a simple route. A Victor airway all the way to my destination, well within spittin' distance, anyway. Nothing the least bit complicated. I have my limit, my route (V-100), my initial altitude, and an expect higher altitude ten minutes after departure. And what can I expect when I get close to the end of V-100? I'll ask for a clearance direct to the Laramie VOR to do the VOR/DME RWY 12 approach into Laramie. I need some VOR approach practice.

V-100 presupposes numerous route segment twists and turns. For the controller to spell out every twist and turn would take all day. Thus, a coded route identifier (V-100) spells out all the moves the pilot is to make during his journey. And should he experience a case of lost communications, all the routes are there to follow, all the minimum altitudes are charted, since once he gets into the vicinity of the Rocky Mountains, he needs to be higher than his expected altitude of 7,000 feet: more like 9,500 feet on his last route segment. All approaches will be available so he can let down. ATC wants no preventable mid-air collisions.

ATC has been known to clear a pilot via direct from NAVAID to NAVAID, forget using the Victor airway system. Or by radar vectors from point to point. All these different routes might presuppose not following the flight plan at all. But you need something to fall back on. So, when you plan your route, like I said, think two-way radio failure. Make sure your flight plan route is something easy to go by, and that ATC, no matter how he routes you, has you either all the way to your destination or back connected to your flight plan route. (Cleared direct or via radar vectors does not presuppose a minimum enroute altitude — because these "routes" are not published. Quizzing ATC is certainly acceptable.)

Cruise Clearance

I'M GOING to create a most incredible scenario, to help you understand IFR clearances better.

This scenario was related to me one day by an air traffic controller when I was an instructor at Fort Rucker, while visiting the Cairns approach control facility at the airfield. I've modified the scenario slightly to make a point.

Per the FAR/AIM: Cruise "... Used in an ATC clearance to authorize a pilot to conduct flight at *any altitude* from the minimum IFR altitude *up to and including the altitude specified in the clearance.* The pilot may level off at any intermediate altitude within this block of airspace. Climb/descent within the block is to be made at the discretion of the pilot. However, once the pilot starts descent and *verbally reports leaving an altitude in the block,* he/she may not return to that altitude *without additional ATC clearance.* Further, it is approval for the pilot to proceed to and *make an approach at destination airport* and can be used in conjunction with:

a. "An airport clearance limit at locations with a standard/special instrument approach procedure. The CFRs (code of federal regulations) require that if an instrument letdown is necessary, the pilot shall make the letdown in accordance with a standard/special instrument procedure for that airport, or

b. An airport clearance limit at locations that are within/below/outside controlled airspace and without a standard/special instrument approach procedure. Such a clearance is NOT AUTHORIZATION for the pilot to descend under IFR conditions below the applicable minimum IFR altitude nor does it imply that ATC is exercising control over aircraft in Class G [uncontrolled] airspace; however, it provides a means for the aircraft to proceed to destination airport, descend, and land IAW applicable CFRs governing VFR flight operations ..."

How the controller derived this scenario from the above written words, I'm not sure. But the way he put it made perfect sense. Imagine if you will a trip from somewhere south of the Canadian border in Minnesota, leaving from Warroad International Memorial (RRT) Airport, the airport just north of the town of Warroad on Muskeg Bay, a part of the Lake of the Woods. The idea is to travel from Warroad, Minnesota, to the Pembina airport (PMB) near the town of Pembina, North Dakota, also still south of the Canadian border, do an approach, land and have dinner with a friend. Then takeoff, go to the Rolla airport (06D) in North Dakota, land and drop off a load of library books. Then depart Rolla for Mohall (HBC) also in North Dakota, land and put the aircraft away for the night. Pembina, Rolla, and Mohall all have a standard instrument approach procedure. Pembina has RNAV (GPS) RWY 33, Rolla has RNAV (GPS) RWY 32, and Mohall has RNAV (GPS) RWY 31.

So, here's the clearance:

"ATC clears Cessna 1234 to the Mohall airport as filed. Cruise 6,000. Contact Minneapolis Center on 134.75. Squawk code 6543. Clearance void if not off by 2318 Zulu. Time now 2200 Zulu."

So, without further ado, let us begin our trip. We depart the Warroad airport, contact Minneapolis Center, he acknowledges, we proceed enroute to our first stop at Pembina, do the approach, land and have dinner. We take off from Pembina, head directly for Rolla, do the approach, land, drop off the books, have a cup of coffee. We take off, head directly for Mohall, and this time announce to ATC that we are leaving 6,000 for the approach at Mohall. ATC acknowledges. He wishes us good night. And reminds us to close out our IFR flight plan. The only time we talked to ATC was on our initial climb out from Warroad and when leaving 6,000 for the approach at our flight plan destination of Mohall. We were never *formally* cleared for any of the approaches into any of our interim stops. How can ATC do this, clear us all the way to Mohall without another radio transmission between us?

The cruise clearance, by definition, authorized it all. On our IFR flight plan, in the route block, we did state that our route was to go from Warroad (RRT) direct to Pembina (PMB) direct to Rolla (06D) direct to Mohall (HBC). At our two interim airports we did an approach without telling ATC we were leaving our cruise altitude, because had we done so, at any time other than at Mohall, our clearance to cruise would have been nullified. In our enroute time we accounted for all our interim stops.

Admittedly, it was a night trip in that part of the country that probably has few IFR flights. If the flight was to last six hours from Warroad to Mohall, just for the heck of it, ATC managed to see that there was to be no other traffic for which you needed to be concerned. So, he cleared you all the way to Mohall with a block altitude of 6,000 down to the minimum appropriate IFR altitude (MEA) for the time frame you requested. Even if Minneapolis Center had handed us off to another controller as we proceeded westward, all we would have said to the new controller is "... this is Cessna 1234, with you cruise 6,000."

Remember, an IFR clearance is designed to keep you clear of all other known IFR air traffic. If there was to be no other IFR traffic along your route of flight, from the MEA to 6,000 feet, this is a perfectly legitimate clearance where you have little to no competition for use of the airspace. Had a request come in from another IFR pilot to be in the same airspace as you, ATC would have called you and amended your cruise clearance. Then wherever you were, you would communicate with ATC to get done what you wanted. Formal, verbally stated clearances and such.

So, what about lost communications? From start to finish there was practically no reason to ever talk to ATC, or receive any further instructions. The initial "cruise" clearance spoke volumes.

So, even if you never make a trip like this, using a cruise clearance, at least you know what the features of a cruise clearance are: a lot of what you can do *said in very few words*. All the implications based on your religiously reading your aeronautical information manual (AIM) coupled with the FARs.

Instrument Approach Procedures (IAPs)

THE IAP, the bread and butter of IFR flight. An organized way of getting safely back on the ground. I can't say enough how important it is to understand instrument approach procedures. For as you leave the higher altitudes that keep you from colliding with obstacles on the ground, the precision aspect of IFR flight becomes readily apparent. There has been an accident or two involving highly trained airline pilots who misread the approach plate, or didn't quite understand the controller's clearance or instructions, and who plowed into the side of a mountain by descending lower than the approach procedure allowed. You simply cannot let this happen. Every step of an instrument approach procedure is designed to get you closer and closer to the ground, so that you can eventually see the airport surface and the runway well enough to land. Each step of an instrument approach procedure will inevitably get you closer to obstacles on the ground as well — closer than safety allows if the procedure is not precisely followed.

The government publication that lays out how an instrument approach procedure is to be designed is called Terminal Instrument Procedures (TERPS). "TERPS criteria have been established for the following instrument procedures: precision approach (PAR, ILS, MLS), non-precision approach (VOR, TACAN, NDB, LOC, ASR), approach with vertical guidance (LDA, LPV, VNAV) required navigation performance (RNP), and for departure procedures. The key considerations for developing terminal instrument approach and departure procedures include but are not limited to: existing obstructions, ground/satellite-based equipment, lighting and aircraft category. TERPS criteria specify the minimum measure of obstacle clearance that is considered by FAA to supply a satisfactory level of vertical protection from obstructions and are predicated *on normal aircraft operations*. Understanding the complexities of Terminal Instrument Procedures is difficult since it is a highly specialized field requiring directed study and/or experience in its applications."

What this says is that the development of an IAP is so complex that it practically requires a PhD. Every aspect of an approach procedure: course lines, minimum altitudes, distances, etc., is critically measured for accuracy and safety. This also means, as previously stated, that every feature of an instrument approach procedure is to be followed exactly (or as nearly so as possible). For example, an LPV DA (descent altitude) of 7,739 feet (MSL) means exactly that, assuming a correctly calibrated altimeter with the right altimeter setting placed in the Kollsman window. An FAA examiner takes a dim view of a pilot going for his instrument rating descending below any published minimum altitude (without legal cause).

It's been since 1988 that I last performed as an instrument instructor. A lot has changed. The GPS approach wasn't yet in existence. The acronyms LPV, LNAV/VNAV weren't in existence, at least not that I can remember. We didn't have GPS receivers on the aircraft we flew. Besides, I want to discuss the intricacies of instrument approach procedures in a broad and general way so that whatever I say doesn't go immediately out of date the moment I say it. This is a "thinking man's" publication. Pilots as a rule don't much like to read dated aviation publications. They don't like when all that's been mentally digested is no longer applicable a month or so later. That is not the jist of this book. "Collision Avoidance: Staying Alive in the National Airspace," was at one time titled "Collision Avoidance: The

Philosophy of Flight in the National Airspace." And it became seriously out of date when all controlled airspace areas were renamed Class A, B, C, etc. Thus, this re-

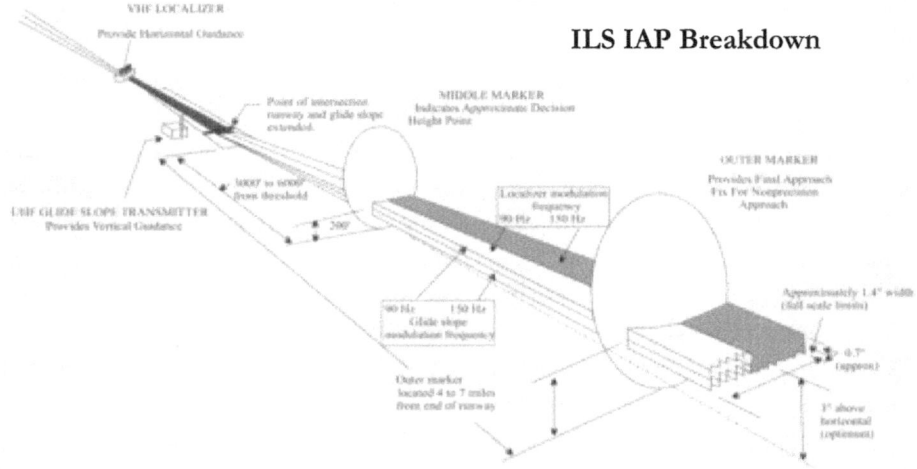

ILS IAP Breakdown

write.

Instrument approach procedures come in two categories: (1) precision vs non-precision; and (2) NAVAID vs ground (radar) controlled. A precision approach procedure is one that provides electronic glideslope (descent angle) information to the pilot, detected by his glideslope receiver; or in the case of a radar-controlled approach, glideslope information passed on to the pilot by the voice commands of a ground controller. (A non-precision approach does not provide glideslope information.) There are three named precision approach procedures: ILS, PAR, and MLS. (The MLS, microwave landing system, was never fully developed due to the introduction of satellite-based systems. This leaves only the other two precision approach procedures to discuss.)

The ILS, instrument landing system, has been around for a good number of years, its development begun as far back as 1929. To keep this narrative short, suffice it to say that performing an ILS approach versus a non-precision approach procedure provides the pilot with the most accurate guidance for approach-end runway alignment (on course, on glidepath). The vertical "on-course" needle in the cockpit is extremely sensitive. A full-scale needle deflection is only 2.5° from center. The horizontal "glideslope" needle indicator is equally sensitive and provides a glideslope angle of approximately three degrees. Remaining at or above this angle assures the pilot of the proper obstacle clearance all the way to touchdown.

There is only one problem with the ILS as a precise instrument approach procedure: the closer to the runway the aircraft becomes the more sensitive course guidance and glideslope information also becomes, to the point that the pilot may tend to overcontrol *in his attempt* to keep both needles centered. That said, the finesse of a steady-handed pilot is a must, in order to take full advantage of such a procedure. Better still, a human pilot must turn himself into an "auto" pilot to do the approach (and himself) justice. When a pilot reaches the decision height (DH) on course and on glidepath, and the runway environment is finally visible, he should be center lined with the straight-in runway at a height above the approach end to do a normal three-degree descent-angle landing. With practice, a pilot can become more and more proficient, but only if he does two things: (1) he must speed up his crosscheck dramatically; and (2) he must think small heading and/or power changes to keep the needles centered. *He must not let his mind wander for an instant.*

The PAR, precision approach radar, normally offered by the military to its pilots, provides precise on course and on glidepath guidance by voice command: a "final" controller sitting before a split radar screen showing an aircraft in relation to the course line and glidepath angle. The final controller sounds something like this: "On course, on glidepath, on course, on glidepath … now going slightly above glidepath, adjust rate of descent. Slightly right of course, turn left heading three five five (assuming a final approach course of 360°). Now on glidepath, now on course, turn right heading three five eight." The controller is constantly talking "… on glidepath, on course, now going below glidepath, stop descent … now back on glidepath … going left of course, turn right heading three five six." Notice the tiny heading changes. During your basic instrument training your instructor should have demonstrated that a roll-in bank angle to the left or right of ten degrees causes the aircraft to automatically change direction five degrees (half the angle of bank), thus during an immediate roll back to wings level the aircraft heading has now changed a total of ten degrees — in and out of a ten-degree bank angle. If you barely nudge the aircraft into a bank, you've changed your heading just a few degrees. During an ILS approach you must act as your own final PAR ground controller, talking yourself down the approach course, your crosscheck about as fast as you can make it. I call it "pinging off the circuit breaker panel."

I offer a thought experiment.

Let's assume you are a highly trained instrument-rated pilot with lots of ILS approach experience. Your aircraft is equipped for flight in IFR conditions. One day you decide to travel VFR 100 miles low level between airports, each with a published ILS instrument approach procedure. The weather is marginal. You are in effect scud-running at around 300 to 400 feet above the ground. Suddenly you punch in—a complete loss of visual reference. The normal tendency (and sometimes it works) is to reduce power and look for any evidence of terra firma. But this time it doesn't work. No sighting of terra firma. What to do? Think. What is the best approach procedure to perform that would get you safely out of the clouds that would preclude hitting an obstruction? The answer: an ILS approach. Why? Well, think how crazy it is to be four hundred feet above the ground, in the clouds, diving and swerving and cajoling the flight controls hoping and praying to see the ground at any minute.

What does an ILS do for you? It does exactly what you are trying to do, short of swerving and diving and cajoling and hoping to see terra firma without hitting anything — *in a controlled way!*

An ILS has you start out around 2,000 to 3,000 feet above the airport surface, then you intercept the glideslope, you are on course, you start your descent, you keep the needles centered, you reach the decision height 200 feet above the earth's surface, then voila! there's the runway, you're perfectly aligned with the centerline, you didn't hit anything, you land — all is good. See the difference between a controlled descent versus a haphazard attempt to reconnect visually with Mother Earth? My sentiments exactly. So, IAPs are either precision or non-precision, and NAVAID assisted or ground-controlled (PAR and ASR).

A NAVAID approach is defined as nothing more than using all required ground-based navigation equipment (transmitters), or GPS "satellite" transmitters, coupled with your onboard navigation receivers to do an instrument approach (procedure). It means that no ground controller plays any part in guiding you down the final approach course to a landing. Since there are only two (that I know of) ground-controlled instrument approaches (the PAR and the ASR — airport surveillance radar), all the rest are NAVAID guided. By name they are SDF, LDA, NDB, VOR, LOC, ILS, RNAV (GPS), etc. The least accurate in terms of course-following and navigating to the missed approach point is the NDB approach. Anyone who has practiced this approach (in VFR conditions) knows that once the MAP is reached (as best you can navigate to it), the likelihood of being where the procedure is designed to take you is almost laughable. The absolute best IAP for accurate course-following (besides the PAR) is the ILS/LOC where the final approach course is designed to have the aircraft center lined with the straight-in runway. If we could only control the aircraft as well as the information provided.

VOR approaches are accurate, but not as accurate as SDF (simplified directional facility), LDA (localizer type directional aid), and GPS (global positioning system) approaches, their course-following information better than decent. Of all instrument approaches, the very best is the PAR, precision approach radar. The final controller tells you every move to make. All you must do is fly the aircraft as well as you can. *You don't even have to think.* (The AIM highlights the SDF and LDA approaches, if you're interested in their understanding.)

Route Segments of an Instrument Approach

ALL IAPs have three components (of necessity) in common: a final approach course, a missed approach point, and missed approach instructions. The final approach course takes you to the missed approach point, or to a landing if the airport environment is adequately visible and you are positioned to land in a safe manner—no desperate nosedives toward the runway. The missed approach instructions are designed to take you up and away to higher, safer altitudes should you be unable to land. The PAR is the simplest of all IAPs. In fact, a PAR is nothing more than a final approach course, a missed approach point, and MAP instructions as described above. All the other approaches are slightly more, if not radically more complex.

An approach procedure begins with a clearance from ATC. When you arrive in the vicinity of your destination, ATC clears you to one of several fixes that begins the approach. It should be said that every part of an instrument approach procedure is a **route segment.** A route segment has three features: a magnetic course, a distance, and a minimum altitude. Outlier fixes are called **feeder fixes.** They take you out of the enroute structure and lead you to the **initial approach fix** (IAF). Or you might be cleared directly to an initial approach fix over which you will begin the approach. Take any instrument approach plate and break the procedure down into its component parts. Each part generally leads to the next part, in descending order of altitude. Remember, each leg of an IAP is designed to get you closer and closer to the ground. The next fix is called the **intermediate fix** (IF). This fix may be an actual place with a name or simply where you happen to intercept the initial approach route which blends into the final approach course after performing a **course-reversal** maneuver. The next fix, then, is called the **final approach fix** (FAF). This is where you begin the final descent to the **missed approach point** (MAP), or rather the FAF is the point at which you start your final descent in the hopes of seeing the runway well enough to land the aircraft. Should you be unable to land, the **missed approach procedure** is the action you take to get back up to higher, safer altitudes. Typically, the missed approach procedure takes you to the **missed approach holding point**. This is exactly like, and in fact is, a clearance limit. When you are cleared for any approach, you are also cleared to do the missed approach procedure to the missed approach holding fix, your official clearance limit. This is true because you cannot simply stop and hold over the missed approach point (still in the clouds) at 200 to 600 feet above the airport surface awaiting a clearance to move on *from that point*. Once the decision is made to do the missed approach procedure, it is performed quickly and without any further blessing from ATC.

If you must perform a missed approach, you must make an announcement to ATC, after you have initiated a climb, after every aspect of your flight is under control. Don't talk until this is so. In other words, talk last.

"Podunk approach, Cessna 1234, executing missed approach."

Since the missed approach holding point is your clearance limit, you don't really need ATC to clear you to it. It's the *implied* clearance limit when you were formally cleared for the approach. But ATC does expect you to tell him what you would like to do next. The MAP holding point is a place to go, if you desire, to collect your wits, to decide your next course of action. If you couldn't land because the atmospheric conditions didn't allow it, what now? One of several courses of action: (1) hold and wait for the weather to improve; (2) hold and prepare yourself for a different approach procedure at the same airport, assuming coming in from another direction might improve your chances of landing; (3) or abandon all hope of landing at your destination and request clearance to your alternate or simply to some other airport.

If your fuel is getting low, you might negate going to your alternate. It may be that you must attempt approach after approach (at the original destination) until you either see the runway and can land, or you bust minimums and hope for the best. At least you'll have crash rescue available, if there, and if needed. You can bust the minimum descent altitude if you declare an emergency. The FAA will only quiz you on your piss poor planning. And maybe cite you accordingly.

The missed approach point (MAP), depending on the procedure, is (1) at the very approach end of the straight-in runway, or very near to it; (2) at the far end of the runway; or (3) offset from the runway, but still somewhere over the airport surface. Wherever it is, that's the place to guide from to go to the missed approach holding point. To guide from any other location, you chance running into some obstacle not accounted for in the design of the procedure. For example, on an ILS approach, when you reach decision height (DH), you'll be damn close to the ground, maybe 200 feet. If the runway is not in sight, a climb straight ahead, then a climbing right or left turn (if required) enroute to the MAP holding point, is the proper course of action. Since an ILS approach is a precision approach, its design is intended to take you practically to the ground aligned perfectly with the straight-in runway. Can't get much better than that. All non-precision approaches have you at the missed approach point generally higher above ground level due to inherent NAVAID inaccuracies.

What is this **course-reversal** maneuver? It is a way to both lose altitude and to maneuver the aircraft for alignment with the final approach course. It is depicted by a **bold procedural track**. One depiction shows a **holding pattern in lieu of a procedure turn.** Another shows a **procedure turn with barb**. Still another is **a high-**

altitude teardrop penetration turn. Yet another shows a **NoPT DME arc**. And finally, simply the **NoPT** route. Because aircraft may approach any and all initial approach fixes from many directions, the course-reversal procedural track is to assist the pilot align with the final approach course. Where it says **NoPT**, this means that the route to the FAF is sufficiently aligned with the final approach course that no course-reversal maneuvering is necessary. **NoPT** means the depicted course-reversal procedural track is not only NOT required — *it is not allowed.*

Thus, the times when a **course-reversal maneuver** is not required (or allowed) fall into several categories. (1) When following a **NoPT DME** arc; (2) when following a **NoPT** route; (3) when performing **timed approaches from a holding pattern** (a little too complicated for discussion here, but you can read up on it in the FAR/AIM); (4) when **cleared straight-in ... approach** (not to be confused with straight-in landing vs circle-to-land); and (5) when **being radar vectored** by ATC to intercept the final approach course of the to-be-performed IAP.

When a **course-reversal maneuver** is necessary to align the aircraft with the final approach course (and is depicted as such), *it must be performed.* When a course-reversal maneuver is not necessary or required to be performed, as per the above paragraph, to do so is contrary to procedure and will bring down the wrath of ATC. For example, to be cleared straight-in ... approach implies that the aircraft is so close to final-approach-course alignment that course-reversal maneuvering is certainly not necessary and is ATC's blessing to forgo following whatever procedural track is depicted. If ATC forgets to say the magic words "... cleared straight-in," just remind him. If he didn't forget, there is a reason he didn't say those key words and he should explain; therefore, do whatever course-reversal maneuver is depicted.

Radar Vectors to Final

SHOULD YOU find yourself in a nonradar environment, all approaches you are likely to perform will require that you follow the entire procedure from start to finish as depicted on the approach plate, depending, of course, on the clearance received. This is called *doing the full approach*. Army pilots who fly regularly in a radar environment will occasionally request to do the full procedure, for practice, forgoing radar assistance. Generally, the time it takes for one aircraft to do the full approach, holding at bay those aircraft in the queue, four and five and more aircraft could have been vectored to final for the same approach and have landed. Vectors to final, in other words, is a way to *expedite the flow of traffic.*

ATC using radar typically guides aircraft, one behind the other, on a left or right downwind (parallel to the final approach course), or on both downwinds, then swings each aircraft around gently until the controller can release each aircraft one at a time to intercept the final approach course, for each pilot to then navigate on his own to complete the *as published* approach. The initial contact to start this procedure comes at a pilot like this: "Cessna 1234, fly heading three six zero, maintain 3,000, vectors for the ILS runway six final approach course." During your time in the traffic pattern, you will hear ATC give instructions to other aircraft ahead of you, thus you can expect similar instructions until you too are released to do your own navigation. Approach clearance comes like this: "Cessna 1234, four miles from [the NDB titled] Ruckr, turn right heading zero three five. Maintain 2,000 until established on the final approach course, cleared ILS runway six approach. Contact tower Ruckr inbound." I call this clearance "the final blast in the ear," after several sets of vector instructions. ATC tells you how far you are from the final approach fix, Ruckr, in this case, what altitude to maintain until established on the final approach course (after which all lower altitudes apply). ATC then formally clears you for the approach. And releases you to the tower operator for landing instructions. Whichever course-reversal procedural track is depicted, you simply overlook. ATC has negated the need for any kind of course-reversal maneuvering.

It's imperative to keep track of your progress on the downwind and to listen carefully to what the controller is telling pilots ahead of and behind you. Should you hear a conflict brewing between what the controller tells you versus what he tells another pilot, you can call and clarify. Controllers are all too human.

The spacing between aircraft is generally three miles laterally and three miles horizontally (or three minutes apart horizontally). And 1,000 feet vertically.

As ATC swings you toward the final approach course, if you see that you are about to cross the course, with no approach clearance yet delivered, maintain last assigned vector heading. DO NOT ARBITRARILY TURN INBOUND. Call ATC and he will explain. It may be that the aircraft ahead of you is having difficulties. ATC might have you continue across the final approach course and do what's called *a box pattern for spacing* (spacing from the aircraft ahead of you). In other words, your initial right (or left) downwind will now turn into the opposite downwind, as you now proceed outbound on the other side of the course. Just stay oriented.

In a busy radar environment, vectors to final is the only way ATC will have you do an approach. On the other hand, should you be heading to a Class B airport, a STAR (standard arrival route) might preclude such vectoring, since the route itself is probably designed to have you aligned (somewhat) with one of the many runways. Once the airport becomes visible to the pilot, and he declares such, the tower operator swings into action to clear him to land.

At Fort Rucker, Cairns approach control had to contend with numerous IFR training helicopters. Instructor pilots were forever coordinating with ATC what to have their student do next. Request for holding instructions was rampant. Requests for a repeat of the last approach was rampant. Requests to allow the student to become mentally lost and to allow him to wander at will to see how long it takes for him to "find himself," was rampant. It was an IFR environment where ATC had to be extraordinarily flexible. It was actually a very dangerous environment for that reason alone. Since training was conducted quite often in clear weather, the chance of a mid-air collision was never better. In IFR conditions, everything became even more serious. Everyone, controller and instructors, had to be at their heightened best.

Other Features of an IAP

IN NO order of importance, the following is a discussion of features of an instrument approach I find necessary to discuss.

An approach procedure may require DME or radar to perform. DME is distance measuring equipment. You can hardly follow or perform a DME arc course-alignment **procedural track** without DME. I think of the DME arc in the same way as being radar vectored to intercept the final approach course. Instead of ATC talking you around, your onboard navigation equipment does it for you. Should a DME arc eventually point you to a **course-reversal procedural track** (holding pattern, procedure turn w/barb, or teardrop), the acronym **NoPT** appears.

Decision height (DH) vs **Minimum Descent Altitude** (MDA). A decision height is associated with a precision approach. An MDA is associated with a non-precision approach. A decision height is so named because it is at this value, as it appears on the altimeter, that the pilot must decide: to either continue descent to land or stop the descent and initiate a climb to perform the missed approach procedure. On course on glidepath, when performing a precision approach, will bring you to the missed approach point. You'll be within 200 feet or less of the ground, aligned centerline with the straight-in runway. If you fear busting through the decision height—you must bust through it slightly to decide whether to continue or not. Your momentum downward cannot suddenly be reversed. It takes time to stop your descent and start a climb.

The MDA is a value *not to go lower than* on a non-precision instrument approach procedure unless the runway environment is adequately visible, and the aircraft is in position to be landed safely. All underlined altitude values depicted on instrument approach plates are not to be discarded until an appropriate time or fix, or upon reaching solid visual conditions. When to descend below any underlined altitude value is a matter of scrutiny. To misread or misinterpret when and where to go below an altitude can have dire consequences. A miscommunication with ATC can be equally disastrous.

A little known or understood feature depicted on an approach plate, located in the profile view, is the bold **V** signifying the acronym VDP, **visual descent point**. Defined in the FAR/AIM as a "... defined point on the final approach course of a non-precision straight-in approach procedure *from which normal descent from the MDA to the runway touchdown point may be commenced*, provided the approach threshold of that runway, or approach lights, or other markings identifiable with the approach end of that runway are *clearly visible to the pilot*." (These are the criteria for descending below the MDA or continuing below the decision height.)

The missed approach point on a non-precision instrument approach procedure, as previously discussed, can be at one of three different locations over the airport: (1) directly over the landing threshold between 350 and 650 feet above the runway (or close to it); (2) at the far end of the runway same height AGL; or (3) displaced away from the runway same height AGL. It appears then that the worst possible place to finally see the airport to land normally and safely is at the MAP. Thus, the VDP, if it can be identified, would be a better missed approach point, because if you go past it and still can't see anything, be prepared to start a climb at the official MAP. Imagine you are in a highspeed aircraft needing all the runway to stop on even if touchdown is at the very approach end. Wouldn't it be nice to see the runway environment well before the missed approach point? It would. The VDP, if recognized, and if the runway is visible, is that place where the aircraft can be descended for landing at a normal 3° approach angle. Simple.

Visual approach vs a **contact approach**. Somewhat alike yet different. The AIM says a **visual approach** is: "An approach conducted on an IFR flight plan which authorizes the pilot to proceed *visually and clear of clouds to the airport*. The pilot must [always] have either the airport or the preceding aircraft in sight. This approach must be authorized and under the control of the appropriate air traffic control facility. Reported weather at the airport must be ceiling at or above 1,000 feet and [a] visibility of three miles or greater."

It is ATC's authorization allowing an IFR aircraft to be flown under visual conditions to the destination airport without the need of following an instrument approach procedure. It is also a way of expediting the flow of IFR traffic. So long as the required visual conditions exist and the pilot can see the airport and/or other air traffic or obstacles to preclude a collision hazard, this clearance usually comes at the end of an IFR flight whereby visual conditions are met long before the need of even doing an instrument approach. Though the pilot may request such a clearance, it is usually ATC that prompts it, to relieve him of the necessity to issue any further instructions. "Cessna 1234, cleared visual approach to the Alamosa airport. Switch to advisory frequency 122.8." Since VFR [weather] conditions are to be assumed, another assumption is that the pilot receiving this kind of clearance will look, see, and avoid other air traffic — that is, maintain proper visual separation.

The AIM says a **contact approach** is: "An approach wherein an aircraft on an IFR flight plan, having an air traffic control authorization, operating clear of clouds with at least 1 mile flight visibility and *a reasonable expectation of continuing to the destination airport in those conditions*, may deviate from the instrument approach procedure and proceed to the destination airport by visual reference to the surface. This approach will only be authorized *when requested by the pilot* [ATC can't initiate] and the reported ground visibility at the destination airport is at least 1 statute mile." If the visibility is that low, and if the distance to the airport is more than a few miles, I think it would be prudent to follow through with the IAP rather than risk a collision with some obstruction. No doubt it is a form of scud-running, hoping to maintain visual contact with the ground. "Cessna 1234, cleared contact approach to the Alamosa airport. Report airport in sight."

When tuned to a **localizer frequency** to perform an ILS approach, note the frequency. All localizer frequencies are within a given range of VHF frequencies (from 108.10 to 111.95). Also note that the ending numbers are always odd, never even. For example, 109.15, 109.3, 109.35, 109.5, 109.55, 109.7, 109.75, etc. No VOR is ever assigned an odd frequency in this range of frequencies. Why? It is to assure that no nearby VOR can ever interfere with any localizer reception by any pilot performing an ILS approach. A nice to know piece of information.

During **radar vectors to final**, it is imperative that the pilot keep oriented in the traffic pattern. Listening to new vector headings issued to other pilots are clues. You must be as interested in what ATC says to other pilots as to what he tells you. When the controller talks a mile a minute, you know he's busy. You can help his workload by paying close attention to his every transmission. ATC's patience wears thin when pilots don't acknowledge new instructions in a timely fashion. **Beware of similar sounding call signs**. Cessna 6074 Alpha is very close to Cessna 6704 Alpha. ATC, to reduce confusion, may abbreviate call signs. From Cessna 6074 Alpha to simply Cessna 74 Alpha and abbreviating 6704 to Cessna 67 Alpha. Anything to eliminate a misunderstanding. Cairns approach control, at Fort Rucker, when I was there, was busier than Chicago O'Hare. Sometimes it was a nightmare listening to every transmission just to ensure no traffic conflict was brewing. Traffic conflicts did brew, more than I liked to think.

Circle-to-land vs **straight-in landing.** Circle to land implies landing on some runway other than the straight-in runway. It implies that the active runway is other than the straight-in runway. It implies that the winds *do not favor* the straight-in runway. A circle-to-land only approach, so named with a letter rather than a number (e.g., VOR Rwy Six approach vs VOR A or B or C approach), implies that the final approach course is offset from all runways by a prescribed number of degrees, thus straight-in minimums will not apply. Circle-to-land minimums are generally higher than straight-in minimums. Now with all that said, if it is critical that you land into the wind, then circle-to-land on the wind-favored runway. If it is not critical, request to land straight-in. This skips the possibility of going back into the clouds during your trip around the traffic pattern to achieve final approach runway alignment. A helicopter pilot does not need to ever circle-to-land. He can align his aircraft into the wind once he is about to touch down; and he doesn't even need to land on a runway; he can land at any clear area on the airport surface.

Altimeter Setting

WHAT ARE the most important set of numbers EVER to read back to ATC exactly, precisely as delivered — without fail?

The answer: the current altimeter setting for the area within which you are flying. Bar none. I can't stress this enough.

Why?

In the Kollsman window there are four digits that can be dialed in that have got to be *right on the money*. If ATC issues the current altimeter for the area you are or will be flying in, it is super imperative that you repeat back exactly the setting he tells you. "Cessna 1234, Podunk altimeter 29.92."

"Podunk altimeter 29.92. Cessna 1234, roger."

Now to reset your altimeter. If your current altimeter setting is 30.42 and you fail to reset it to the lower value of 29.92, how far off will your AGL altitude be as you fly your assigned MSL altitude? The difference between 30.42 and 29.92 is .50 which equates to a whopping 500 feet. The breakdown is this:

.01 difference equals 10 feet
.10 difference equals 100 feet
1.0 difference equals 1,000 feet

This means that if you fail to lower your altimeter to the proper value of 29.92 from 30.42, you'll be 500 feet closer to the ground than intended. Or off your assigned altitude by 500 feet, lower than intended. Never fail to lower your altimeter setting when ATC tells you the current setting, especially from a higher value to the lower value. In the opposite vein, to fail to raise your altimeter setting by .01 or .10 or 1.0, has you off your proper above ground altitude by 10 feet, or 100 feet, or

1,000 feet respectively, or, in this case, you'll be higher in altitude than intended. Lower by 10, 100, or 1,000 feet than intended can have you plowing into the ground (not knowing what hit you) as the ultimate surprise—for about a split second.

From high to low, LOOKOUT below!

Let's see if we can visualize this a little better. The high-end tolerance of our altimeter is plus or minus 75 feet, or .075, checked and recalibrated by someone qualified to do so. We can cursory check the altimeter ourselves, and should do so periodically.

We'll make this simple. Our aircraft is hangered at an airport that is exactly at sea level, zero feet field elevation. Barometric pressure never really stays the same, changing from day to day, sometimes more often. One day we get in the cockpit and adjust the altimeter to the field elevation of zero. We note the reading in the Kollsman window is 30.00 with a zero-field elevation indication. We call the tower and the operator states the current altimeter to be 30.00. From this we can assume that our altimeter is calibrated perfectly—no error.

We come back the next day, get in the cockpit and note that with 30.00 still dialed in the altitude reading is a plus 100 feet, or 100 feet above the field elevation of zero. We adjust the altimeter back to the field elevation of zero and note the value in the Kollsman window is now 29.90. The tower operator gives the current altimeter setting of 29.90. Great! Still no error. Had we not adjusted the altimeter downward to 29.90 from 30.00, what would we have had to do with the aircraft to get a field elevation reading of zero? Answer: drive the aircraft into the ground by 100 feet! *From high to low, lookout below.* In the opposite vein, had the altimeter read a minus 100 feet with 30.00 still di-

Pressure Sensitive Altimeter

aled in the Kollsman window, what adjusted altimeter setting would give us a field elevation of zero? It would be 30.10, assuming still an error-free altimeter. Had we not adjusted the reading in the Kollsman window, what must we physically do now with the aircraft to get a field elevation of zero? We would have to suspend the aircraft 100 feet above the ground. Thus, to not reset the altimeter to a higher barometric pressure reading would put us higher than we are supposed to be.

I sure hope this makes sense. It is such a critical concept. To fail to **lower** the Kollsman window reading from some higher value is to be **lower** than you really want to be above ground level. To fail to **raise it** puts you **higher** than you really want to be.

From high to low, LOOKOUT below!

To further cement this concept (and assuming an error-free altimeter), let's place ourselves on an ILS approach where when we typically reach decision height (of whatever MSL altitude value) we should find ourselves right around 200 feet above the ground.

If current altimeter is 29.90, but we still have dialed in the Kollsman window 30.00 (an altimeter setting good for some other location), instead of 29.90, when we reach the MSL decision height, how high above the ground will we be now? We failed to lower the altimeter by .10, which puts us closer to the ground by 100 feet. Lower than the proper 200 feet AGL. Can you imagine being in the clouds 100 feet above the ground still unable to see the runway? What if the new altimeter setting was 30.10 and we kept the old setting of 30.00 in the Kollsman window? At the MSL decision height, how high would we be above the ground? Instead of 200 feet, we'd be 100 feet higher, at 300 feet AGL. Had we gotten down 100 feet lower, we might have been able to see enough of the runway to land.

From low to high, TOO high!

Anytime ATC relays the current altimeter setting, you must read it back verbatim. If ATC told you the wrong setting, he will catch *his* error. If you read back a wrong setting, he will correct *your* error.

If you are equipped with a radar altimeter, so much the better. This type of altimeter gives you an exact height above ground level reading when within 500 feet of the surface. It is not supposed to be barometric pressure sensitive since what it does is transmit a signal from aircraft to ground, and the bounce-back signal to the receiver accurately tells the pilot his *real elevation* above ground level.

Radar Altimeter

Imagine two pilots holding over the same VOR. One is assigned to 4,000 feet MSL and the other is to be at 3,000 feet MSL. If the pilot above has his altimeter set incorrectly, whereby he failed to lower the setting from 30.00 to 29.50, and the one below failed to reset his altimeter from 29.00 to 29.50, how far apart would they technically be? **Zero feet**. The one above would be 500 feet lower than he is supposed to be, and the one below would be 500 feet higher than he's supposed to be, all while holding over the *same NAVAID.*

One last thought. If your altimeter is off by the maximum allowed of 75 feet, you need to somehow take that into consideration, especially when performing a precision approach, like an ILS or PAR. In other words — think about it but not so much that you compound the error by making an *improper* adjustment.

Holding Instructions

ATC HOLDING instructions can be confusing. There is a way to resolve the confusion. To hold south of some fix or north of it or southwest of it, the thing to remember is that it is the **course line** that is south or north or southwest, not the bulk of the racetrack pattern. Example #1, with the dot being the transmitter, and the arrow aiming toward the dot after a teardrop entry, it appears that the bulk of the pattern lies east (& south) of the fix, but this is not how a clear-

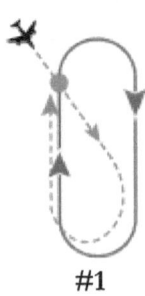

#1

ance to hold will come to you: "Cessna 1234, hold south of the NDB on the 360° course TO, right turns. EFC at ..." If ATC told you to do left turns, the bulk of the pattern would appear to be west (& south) of the fix versus as it shows. In example #2, this is a depiction of holding east of a fix with right hand *standard* turns. The course TO would be west or 270°. The bulk of the pattern relative to the holding fix is north (& east). If turns were to the left the bulk of the holding pattern would be south (& east). Here's the clearance: "Cessna 1234, hold east of the fix, right turns, EFC at ..." Here's example #3: "Cessna 1234, hold northeast of the VOR, right turns, EFC at ..." The course to the VOR appears to be 238°, approximately. The course line itself, however, lies most assuredly to the northeast. The bulk of the holding pattern does lie north and east of the fix. With left hand turns, however, the bulk would lie *more south and east.* So, the purpose of this discussion is to inform you that IT IS THE HOLDING COURSE LINE that is east of or south of or northwest of and NOT THE BULK OF THE HOLDING PATTERN.

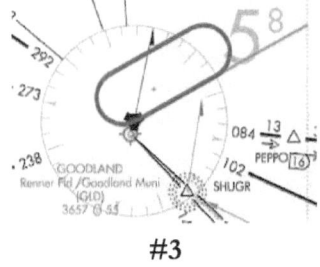

#3

Much mental gymnastics goes into deciding what kind of entry to make. Direct, parallel, or teardrop. I maintain that what it first appears to be is generally what the entry *should be*. The arrow to the left implies a direct entry; the arrow at the bottom implies teardrop; and the right arrow implies parallel. In other words, rather than go through too much mental anguish, why not

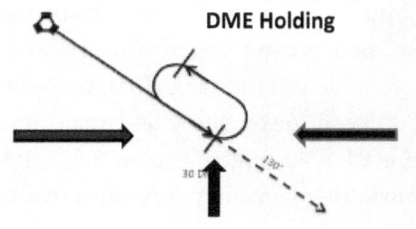

DME Holding

make it easy. What does it LOOK LIKE you should do? Of course, when in doubt cross the fix and turn to the outbound heading. Fly for one minute then turn the shortest number of degrees back to the fix.

There will be a time or two when you get "lost in holding." Not to worry, you have not suddenly become magically transported to Russia or China or Timbuktu. You probably haven't even crossed any state lines. Navigate back to the holding fix as best you can and start the procedure over. If nothing else at least parallel the inbound holding course. The course is either left or right of your current position. ATC doesn't really care whether you fly a perfect holding pattern. It could look like a tossed salad, a bowl filled with a savory angel hair pasta, or a can of fishing worms. Stay at least close to the holding fix so as not to wander too far away from the airspace you've been allotted. It takes about four to five turns in holding to nail down the winds. By then ATC will probably have cleared you onward.

Holding is an organized way to stop moving forward. Modify the procedure as you see fit. Let common sense rule.

Listen to ATC

ONE WAY to study IFR communications is to buy a VHF scanner radio and tune it to a nearby tower frequency, or approach control channel, or ARTCC and at least listen to how pilots transmit back to ATC. Better still, go to an air traffic control facility on a visitor pass, sit and watch what controllers do at their station(s). Just as VOR frequencies and ILS (localizer) frequencies and tower frequencies remain the same through the years, air traffic control clearances and instructions and practices also remain relatively the same. A route clearance can hardly be any different than it is; vectors to final can hardly be altered than what's been proven to work. Delve into ATC's plan for handling a lost communications situation. The more you understand their protocol in that regard, the better your frame of mind will be should two-radio failure occur. Keep control of the aircraft and of yourself and fly your last assigned clearance. Tune to any NAVAID that has voice capability, whereby ATC can talk to you through a navigation transmitter channel. Your response (as previously discussed) can be squawk IDENT, or he might tell you to turn left or right briefly so that he can monitor your turns on radar, as a signal that you are receiving his messages.

My nine years spent at Fort Rucker, listening to ATC morning, afternoon, and into the night, the sameness of it all became rather boring except when the weather reared its ugly head. Before I became an instrument instructor, I classed myself as barely IFR qualified. In other words, it took two years teaching, mind you, to say I was as knowledgeable as anyone should be after training and passing an initial IFR check ride, to finally be equal to my IFR rating. Seventy percent of the pilots that flew with the Alabama Army National Guard out of Montgomery, Alabama, were Fort Rucker instructors of one stripe or another. Some were involved in initial student training in the TH-55A, others taught Huey transition, others instructed in the use of night vision goggles, and still others taught low-level navigation and tactics. Some of the other thirty percent were not instructors but were Vietnam vets who had civilian jobs quite apart from flying. Though all guard pilots were required to pass an annual instrument check ride, those that weren't instrument instructors hated wearing that damn hood and sweating through an hour and a half of torture trying hard not to appear as spastic as they were long ago going through the flight training program before deploying to Vietnam. I tried to get a few of them, when we flew together, to file an IFR flight plan and deal with ATC on our way to summer camp, but they wanted nothing to do with it. A lot of army pilots hate to talk to ATC. I have long since understood their misgivings which were the same as mine when I went through the same training. IFR flying is practically all mental. Your brain housed in a cockpit surrounded by white cloud, nothing to look at but the instruments, gauges, radio dials, your being always on edge. So, I've formulated a better training methodology.

How to Improve Instrument Flight Training

IF IFR flying is ten percent aircraft control and ninety percent thinking, visualizing, deciding, listening, orienting, navigating, communicating, it seems the worst time to introduce the ninety percent thinking is directly after the ten percent learning basic instruments, the stuff of aircraft control. Now's the time for table-talk. Lots of table-talk. A month of it, with pages of blank paper to graph scenarios. Time now for the instructor to teach thinking, to teach clearances, to talk students through an instrument approach procedure, lots of them. Then have the student do the same. If a student can't talk his way through a procedure how can he be expected to fly his way through it as he struggles with the controls?

I accumulated 2,900 hours of three-axis, full-motion instrument flight simulator (SFTS) time at Fort Rucker. There were four devices to one platform controlled by a pair of console operators. Each cockpit device resembled that of a Huey helicopter. The windshield was opaque. Behind the two upfront cockpit seats was a jump seat for the instructor. On a wall above the instructor's seat was a CRT monitor. As the student progressed through imaginary space, his flight path left an electronic trace across the screen. Course lines familiar to the Fort Rucker training area were superimposed on the screen. This allowed the instructor to note how well the student intercepted a course, how well he navigated to intersections, how well he performed within a holding pattern at a NAVAID. I had a "freeze" button to stop simulator motion, to then show the student where he was going wrong in his reaction to a clearance. The student would turn in his seat and look back at the monitor as I explained the situation. I never liked for the student to get so wildly off course in his thinking that it was impossible for him to mentally catch up. So, once I knew the student was hell-bent on going haywire, I stopped him midstream to steer him right. Later, after he'd gotten the message more than a few times, I'd let him "get lost" to see if he could recover on his own. In the aircraft, when the student got confused, I'd take the controls and have him watch me do the task at hand. No freeze button in the aircraft.

Every two months we were assigned two new students. The students had just barely transitioned into the Huey before leaping headlong into instrument instruction. They were overwhelmed with a large cockpit with triple the number of gauges and doodads to fuss with after their initial helicopter training in the TH-55A. They didn't have any pilot-in-command time to fall back on. Instrument training was a giant leap into the fire. So, we instructors became expert at holding their hands.

Sadly, we instructors never did have adequate table-talk time. We were hamstrung by the students' extremely tight training schedule, the flying part seemingly a minor interruption. We did our best. At the end of their training cycle, they took their check ride. Most passed, if they weren't too spastic during their check flight being with someone other than their babysitting instructor. So much information to cram into their heads, so little time.

To think and fly at the same time is very difficult. For a student to listen to instruction while at the same time be at the controls, it's a wonder he could retain maybe ten percent of it. This is where adequate table talk comes in handy. The more the merrier. Until it sinks in.

The aim of this book is for light bulbs to go off in your head one after the other. I therefore challenge your instructor to sit with you day and night reiterating all the nuances of every conceivable procedure. Then get in the aircraft and fly and think at the same time.

Orientation

WHERE ARE we in space and how do we know it? GPS may be today's pilot godsend but what if it goes on the blink. Can you pinpoint yourself on a low altitude IFR enroute chart? What if radar also goes on the blink? Do you know what time you arrived at your last checkpoint and can you give an estimate to your next IFR fix? In a nonradar environment, ATC will occasionally ask you what radial you are crossing emanating from some nearby VOR. This is how he keeps track of your progress, by calculating your groundspeed and when you should arrive at where you are going. Distance divided by rate equals time, thus ETA to your next checkpoint.

From any nearby NAVAID or fix, you are FROM it by some bearing. If you tune to first one then another NAVAID, where the bearings cross is *supposedly* where you are. As confirmation, choose a third NAVAID (if one is available) to nail it down. Before you do that, first decide what bearing you should see from that third NAVAID, so that you don't arbitrarily accept what it indicates. You could be wildly off. If you are wildly askew maybe you didn't gauge the bearings from the first two NAVAIDs properly.

When I flew EMS, I was constantly checking my progress using my VFR sectional chart along with my GPS receiver. I'd tune to nearby VORs and NDBs. My mind raced: did I have enough fuel? We could never carry a full load of fuel due to aircraft weight limitations. Crewmembers were supposed to be weight limited. Occasionally they hired a grossly overweight paramedic, not very often.

After a fashion, we pilots became so familiar with our area of operation that prominent landmarks were easily recognizable. Highways, towns, water towers, radio towers, power lines, high rise buildings, hilltops. At night the lights of small towns helped guide us. Clusters of well-lit radio towers were a dead giveaway. The rotating beacons of airports along our route assisted.

It seems that there are more RNAV (GPS) instrument approaches than VOR or NDB or ILS approaches. Good or bad, I don't know. You can't rely only on knowing how to use the GPS. RNAV approaches rely heavily on waypoints. All well and good but one day you might be confronted with an NDB approach and a **procedure turn with barb** to perform course reversal, where the NDB transmitter is located on the airport surface (called a terminal approach). Do you know how to do an approach like that?

Should the glideslope feature of an ILS go belly up are you prepared to revert to the *localizer only* portion of the approach?

Don't you just hate lectures?

Target Fixation

I HAVE been so focused on what I thought was my airport of intended landing, only to find myself looking down while passing directly over it. LOOK AROUND! Your projected destination may be closer than you think or not at all where you think. A nice stream of lights at night could be a busy freeway and not the runway lights or approach lights of an airport. Tall radio towers have guywires leading to the ground. To focus on the tower ONLY is to forget the guywires. Flight down the middle of a canyon or along a narrow valley can prove fatal if the pilot doesn't see the long spans of high-voltage power lines.

To give an example of costly target fixation, Eastern Air Lines Flight 401 was a scheduled flight from New York to Miami. On December 29, 1972, Flight 401, a Lockheed L-1011-1 Tristar aircraft, crashed into the Florida Everglades, causing 101 fatalities. The pilots and the flight engineer, two of 10 flight attendants, and 96 of 163 passengers died; 75 passengers and crew survived. *The crash occurred while the entire cockpit crew was preoccupied with a burnt-out landing gear indicator light. They failed to notice that the autopilot had inadvertently been disconnected and, as a result, the aircraft gradually lost altitude and crashed.*

Target fixation also occurs during flight instruction, when the flight instructor focuses on the navigation instruments, teaching and guiding, neglecting his scan outside the cockpit. In 1967 a mid-air collision occurred between two instrument training helicopters in clear visibility while I was a student at Fort Rucker. Four people died, one of them was a classmate whose wife had recently been in a bad car accident and was paralyzed from the waist down. Two small children were left to the care of extended family members.

Sterile Cockpit

WHAT THE hell is a *sterile cockpit*? Landing and takeoff, perhaps the two busiest times in an aircraft, are when distractions must be kept to a minimum. No joke telling. No playing footsies. No ass-grabbing. Your passengers must be forewarned prior to those times so that it becomes habit. In a helicopter, the most vulnerable times are during liftoff and landing, when the aircraft during takeoff hasn't yet reached a decent airspeed to affect a limited injury but survivable autorotation should the only engine quit. Same during landing, that time when the helicopter becomes slower and slower right before touchdown. An engine failure seventy-five feet up, if it doesn't kill you, will likely break your back. Crew and passengers should be buckled in, and quiet as little church mice, so that the pilot can concentrate.

An instructor pilot friend of mine long ago, who taught in the instrument flight examiner (IFE) course, experienced a Huey helicopter engine failure in the clouds at 6,000 feet MSL. The two rated student aviators in the cockpit seats were Huey instructors, and knew exactly what to do. My IP friend, who was seated in the jump seat, did his best to assist, making emergency radio calls, calling out performance instrument readings, etc. The latest weather report was ceiling 200 feet and visibility 3 miles. Now all they had to do was hope and pray that when they broke out of the clouds at 200 feet AGL, there was a place to land directly to their front, that there would be no power lines to avoid or a radio tower and guywires to dodge. They were blessed. There was no structural damage to the helicopter. The landing was perfect, in an open, freshly plowed field. The trio had just the right target fixation: making sure the aircraft was under control, the rotor rpm was in the green range, the airspeed at 60 to 70 knots. And I'm guessing that light-hearted bantering was kept to an absolute minimum—like there was none. A perfectly sterile cockpit.

EMS Helicopter Flying

I DON'T know what I expected. In late May 1988 I interviewed for a pilot position with Rocky Mountain Helicopters, in a motel room in Daleville, Alabama, outside one of the Fort Rucker main gates. I had acquired close to 6,200 flight hours,

was well qualified in instruments, and was very interested in this type of flying. Jeff Lewis (not his real name), the interviewer, a pilot himself, explained that Rocky had to comply with a FAA mandate to fill each of its contracts with a fourth pilot to satisfy crew rest requirements. At the time Rocky Mountain Helicopters was the largest purveyor of EMS helicopters, pilots, and mechanics in the United States.

To get a feel for what I was in for, so I could make an informed decision, Jeff sent me to Hartford Hospital in Hartford, Connecticut,

BK-117

where I was to ride along with the on-duty pilot in a BK-117 helicopter. I was given a sleeping room, and when a call came, I was to go quickly to the ground-level landing pad, strap myself into the left cockpit seat, and observe the actions of the pilot and medical crew. The BK-117 is a twin-engine machine, and it seemed to take forever to get both engines online for liftoff. There was no panic, just casual confident efficiency.

My first flight was at night, a bad auto accident involving a young mother enroute somewhere. The medical crew continued CPR protocol all the way to the hospital. The pilot shut the aircraft down, he and I went into the ER, and I watched with wide-eyed fascination as the trauma team did all they could to revive her. Within half an hour or so, the young woman was pronounced dead. A sheet was pulled over her, the team walked away, and I pondered the death of this person covered and lying there all alone, wondering about her family, her husband and children. I was puzzled. Wasn't performing CPR a sure sign that the victim was going to survive? Apparently not. Directly after that, with the image of the covered body still imprinted on my mind, another call came, one that was to take us toward the Long Island Sound coastline. In the near distance we saw storm clouds and bright lightning flashes. The pilot advised the crew that the weather didn't look so good and that he was turning back, that he was now declining the flight. They said that was fine with them, they had a lot of medical charting to do. For some reason, that too seemed odd. In Vietnam, we pilots didn't let the weather stop us from continuing to help whoever was in trouble.

I went on two more flights, both during the day. On the first flight, we landed at a hospital in Bridgeport. The landing pad, next to a building, seemed no bigger than a postage stamp, but the BK's tight profile allowed for such a confined space. The second flight took us to Poughkeepsie, in New York state. This time our landing zone was in the middle of a side street near the hospital. Firefighters were there to secure the LZ from automobile traffic. The pilot conversed with the firemen, telling them how much he appreciated their help. The pilot told me how important it was to always validate emergency personnel who facilitated the landing zone. That was my introduction.

What I remember most was how calm each pilot was, how easily they threw switches, pressed buttons, handled each engine start with self-assurance, modulating the throttle to ensure no engine temperature limitation was exceeded. Their cockpit organization seemed casual, yet efficient. Of the three pilots, only one was a Vietnam vet, who had been severely wounded taking a round through his jaw. His face was slightly disfigured; he took his appearance with casual indifference.

I informed Jeff Lewis that I would be glad to join Rocky Mountain Helicopters. I was hired and he arranged for me to go to Provo, Utah, Rocky's headquarters, for training and indoctrination. There I met the administrators, all Vietnam vets. It was like old homecoming week. 1988 was thirteen years after the fall of Saigon. Flight for life helicopter flying is sanctioned by FAR Part 135, unscheduled air taxi service. There were others there for training, all of them Vietnam veterans. Rocky was gathering the old guard, experienced pilots still with lots of piss and vinegar to do in the civilian world what they had basically done in Vietnam — to fly at a moment's notice to wherever they were asked to go. Minus being shot at.

The French-built SA 316B helicopter, nicknamed the Allouette, was an odd machine, many referring to it as "the John Deere tractor of the skies." It was designed for high altitude work in the European alps. The engine was started by flipping a switch. Then at a certain engine rpm, next came engaging the rotor system. In the Huey, the main rotor blades, as viewed from inside the cockpit, turn clockwise. In the Allouette, the main rotors turn in the opposite direction, which meant working the anti-torque pedals counter to what I was accustomed. The very first civilian "flight for life" helicopter in the United States was based in Denver at St. Anthony Central Hospital back in the early 70s, and it was there the Allouette III made its debut, the right high-altitude aircraft for the surrounding mountains. The top speed of the thing was around 90 knots. It had almost unlimited power. And it was *odd-looking*, an airframe with the afterthought of an engine placed behind the rotor mast, completely exposed, no protective engine cowling. Compared to the BK-117, which was enclosed, bulky and dramatic, the Allouette III, viewed as an EMS helicopter, didn't seem sophisticated enough for its mission — that of saving lives.

Allouette III

After my training, I said goodbye to my wife and two daughters in Alabama and flew to Pittsburgh, Pennsylvania, where I linked up at a two-helicopter contract, there to become more familiar with the mission. Again, when a call came, I strapped myself into the left cockpit seat of still another BK-117 to observe pilot and crew. It was August. A haze the color of split-pea soup blanketed the area, the visibility easily less than five miles.

Johnstown, Pennsylvania

MY ORIENTATION concluded, the mechanic on contract at Conemaugh Valley Memorial Hospital (CVMH) in Johnstown, drove me to the pilot quarters which sat across the street from the hospital. The Allouette was parked on a rooftop helipad eight stories up. I learned that CVMH was one of three Johnstown city hospitals. Suitcase in hand I stood inside the door of the pilot quarters surprised to see

Jeff Lewis, the pilot on duty, when the pager attached to his belt went off. It was a hospital transfer request from one of the Johnstown sister hospitals to Allegheny General, the same hospital I oriented at in Pittsburgh. Jeff asked if I wanted to take the flight. I said, "Sure. Why not." Jeff, I learned, was higher in the chain of command than I thought, supervising four other contracts in the New England area, filling in when needed, which was why he was there to greet me: he was the current relief pilot because the contract was short two pilots, not just one.

During my training in the Allouette, I hadn't started it but four times. My familiarity with this odd helicopter was all of three hours of flight time. When the army trains you in a new helicopter, they take a month and twenty-five flying hours, including daily ground school, to get you up to speed. In other words, the army manages to *cram into four weeks* what it apparently takes the civilian flying world to do in three or four days.

Jeff introduced me to the medical crew, two nurses, both appearing in their early forties. They raised their eyebrows and agreed to have me, someone they knew not at all, take the flight request. They were already buckled in and visibly impatient. I did a quick walkaround, positioned myself inside the cockpit, and hoped like hell I could get the Allouette started without a hitch. Jeff stood next to the open cockpit door and watched.

The SA 316B's landing gear were three small wheels. I had been warned repeatedly about ground resonance for which the aircraft was prone should the pilot be hesitant in either lifting off or grounding the landing gear. "Ground resonance is an imbalance in the rotation of a helicopter rotor when the blades become bunched up on one side of their rotational plane and cause an oscillation in phase with the frequency of the rocking of the helicopter on its landing gear." Admittedly, not much of an explanation. And this technical description does not say how the imbalance can literally vibrate the helicopter into a pile of twisted rubble. To compensate, the pilot must not hesitate picking the ship up to a three-foot hover on liftoff, or setting down from a hover. No landing-gear toe-tapping. And I still wasn't comfortable with the rotors going the "wrong" way.

The sister hospital where the patient was located was about a mile from CVMH. I found it easily with the help of the two nurses. I saw the winds were coming from the southeast so I aimed the ship in that direction, toward a rooftop landing pad. Several hospital staff were there to assist the crew with their equipment. I noted also a man severely dressed in business suit and tie. After I shut the engine down, and the rotors had come quickly to a complete stop using the rotor brake, he advanced, and with a disturbed voice, asked why I hadn't approached the pad the way the other pilots did, which would have been downwind. I explained my reasoning but the scowl on his face remained. This episode would be one of many such occurrences over a fourteen-year career where a lay person unfamiliar with flying would chastise me on what I thought was good pilot planning and judgment. I would also learn over time that when you have four pilots at a contract, each would have a slightly different way of doing the same thing. Usually the medical crew adjusted, but hospital administrators were notorious quibblers when it came to things done a certain way.

The flight to Pittsburgh was uneventful. I cleared the mountains and headed west. Pittsburgh was about fifty-five air miles away and because on this day the visibility was unusually void of haze, I spotted the city in the distance right away. I figured the flight would be a piece of cake. I knew the exact location of Allegheny General, at the confluence of the Ohio River, the Allegheny River, and the Monongahela, the reason Steeler stadium was called Three Rivers Stadium.

Both BK-117s were parked in their spots. I landed, shut down, the crew and hospital personnel offloaded the patient, then I dragged the fuel hose over to refuel. My first hospital transfer was a success, at least in my mind. I wasn't to learn of the controversy I created until I returned to Johnstown, and this was presented to me after another transfer request, which I also took, again to Allegheny General. This time the patient came from the Conemaugh Valley hospital. Two flights under my belt and my unpacked bags were still sitting on the floor in the living room of the pilot quarters when I returned.

It was now mid-afternoon, so Jeff decided we should fly to the airport and around the city for an orientation, the very thing that should have been done before my first official EMS flight. In less than four hours of flight time, I had six engine starts. It seems that all helicopter pilots can jump into any helicopter and fly it, if someone gets it started. The number of starts learning a new helicopter, though, is just as important as the number of flight hours, landings and takeoffs. In other words, monitoring the engine temperature during a start, shutting the fuel off immediately should a hot-start be imminent, motoring the ignition trigger for cooling—is key.

Jeff suggested that I get cozy with the medical crew so they could learn to trust me and have confidence in my flying skills. He advised that I banter with them during a flight, when they weren't focused on a patient. I frowned and thought that perhaps a quiet, reclusive pilot was not reliable. In that this type of flying was new to me, it wasn't in my mind to cave to light banter when I should be focused on the gauges, on potential forced landing areas, on orientation. I had always been serious about flying, not taking anything for granted. As an aircraft commander in Vietnam, I insisted that my co-pilot maintain his chosen airspeed and altitude, and not lollygag through the air as I had known other ACs to tolerate. During my time in Johnstown (from August to November 1988), of the nine flight nurses (all women), two of them declared a pure hatred for me because I was so serious. I suppose the other pilots were more lighthearted, more jovial. I just couldn't be that way. I likened a helicopter as an assembly of mostly rotating parts traveling miraculously close together seeking the first opportunity to become *disassembled – or broke*. It was my intent to be ready for anything – screw the medical crew's sensibilities. (I was told by one pilot years later that he considered the medical crew as the only hazardous material, aside from medical O2, that he carried.) I thought this true in some cases but not all. It only took one or two prima donnas to affect the rest.

Aside from using VORs and NDBs, and a VFR sectional to guide by, LORAN, the acronym for long range navigation, was another onboard navigation receiver. I learned that "aircraft location is determined by the intervals between signal pulses received from widely spaced, land-based radio transmitters." It was a navigation tool that I hadn't been trained to operate or program properly, and my attempt at self-teaching left me more frustrated than confident in its use. It was so easy to trundle along entering a set of coordinates only to be unable to backtrack to correct an error. I recall my first scene flight. I was given a set of coordinates and told that the patient was a man who had somehow become mangled by the machinery he operated. As usual the skies where hazy, barely four miles visibility. As I flew over hilly terrain northeast of Johnstown, I remember praying that the coordinates were good, that I had entered them correctly, and that if they weren't right on that I could still find where the patient was located. The coordinates got me miraculously to the exact right spot. But there was a glitch. I couldn't land at the scene due to the uneven terrain. The idea of dynamic rollover was a helicopter pilot's other worst nightmare (there were so many). So, I flew up hill away from the scene until I saw what looked like level terrain. I landed and watched as the victim's work partners slowly brought him uphill to the helicopter carried in the bucket of a frontend loader.

The man lay in a pool of his own blood. The two flight nurses took control and continued CPR. They got him loaded on the stretcher and then slid into the helicopter. In the Allouette, the patient is positioned behind the pilot's seat. The two crewmembers were seated side by side to my left, their backs faced in the direction of flight. I could see out of the corner of my eye the nurses working on the patient. I automatically knew this man was in serious trouble. I was still naïve enough to believe that because CPR was in progress that the patient was still alive and would survive. Again, I was wrong. He bled completely out on the flight to the hospital. In fact, the two nurses were certain he was dead before they even got to him.

While I was in Vietnam a call came from an American advisor who had seven severely wounded Vietnamese soldiers that needed immediate medical evacuation. I was in the area and answered the call. Four of the less critically wounded were loaded first followed by three whose abdomens were split open with their guts hanging out. I was met at the Tra Vinh province city airfield by a Vietnamese ambulance crew who braved the wretched mass to determine which of the men were salvageable. They carried off the four that were obviously still alive leaving three dead on the cabin floor, their bodies seemingly floating in blood. The Vietnamese medics refused to offload them so my door gunner and I did the chore, dumping their mangled corpses by the side of the runway. Back at the Soc Trang airfield I set our ship down next to the control tower where a crash-rescue firetruck was standing by. The Vietnamese firemen hosed the inside of the ship with several hundred gallons of water.

The Allouette was similarly steeped in blood. At the time, too, I didn't realize the corrosive properties of this cherry red, life-serving liquid. Blood seeped (at times dripped) from beneath the ship for two days before the underbelly was exposed and inspected, and cleaned thoroughly.

Conemaugh Valley Memorial Hospital was associated with big Pittsburgh Allegheny General as a sort of little sister, a location for the third helicopter of a two-helicopter hospital contract — the Allouette probably thought not a real helicopter. Somehow a spat between the two hospital administrations caused the decision to rid CVMH of its Allouette. The medical crew was more than devastated. A job they had grown to love was slowly being ripped from them. Therefore, and because I wasn't the jovial sort, they were at times noticeably irritated with me. Long before the helicopter was to depart, the contract had been reduced to two pilots, myself and the lead pilot. By the end I had pulled thirty straight days without a break. The lead pilot, whose family was in the area, opted to do the night duty so that he could spend time during the day with his wife and two boys. I was never happier to leave a place (other than Vietnam) than Johnstown, Pennsylvania, my introduction to EMS flying a disheartening experience in so many ways. Not only was the weather, mostly due to fog, especially at night, foul and unpredictable, but the Alleghenies felt treacherous, their hilltops and valleys, the danger of flying among them at night as fearful as the terrain had been in Vietnam. The LORAN navigation system, at least the receiver in the cockpit, was still a puzzle to me, and its land-based transmitters were prone to flights of irregular inconveniences. Even when I programmed the LORAN correctly, I was lucky to get within a quarter-mile of a location.

Johnstown, is in the heart of coal and steel mill country. Fine coal and metal particulate float unseen through the air, a key ingredient for the formation of fog. One night, after dropping a patient off at Allegheny General, I noted that the air had a peculiar look to it on the way back to home base. The spine of the Alleghanies lie directly west of Johnstown. The city rested cradle-like as in a bowl. The Johnstown airport sat east of the hospital on a plateau above the city. The visibility at the airport was clear, I could easily see the flashing airport beacon. As we overflew the hospital and the city, all I could see below was a faint glow through a dense carpet of white-gray cloud. Thus, I elected to land at the airport. Directly after landing, with the blades tied down, I was walking with the crew toward the terminal building when I happened to glance back at the aircraft. What had been clear skies was now ham and pea soup. The helicopter had become invisible within ten minutes after landing. I had seen at night on more than one occasion the sky having that certain dreaded look. It was bad enough that I didn't have that much familiarity with the area after dark, but haze, the potential for fog, and the black of night do not go well together for almost any reasonable expectation of decent visibility.

I did have one comfortable, beautiful flight along the Alleghenies to Williamsport. The skies were clear, not a hint of haze or moisture. It was a one-hundred-and-thirty-mile trip under the most ideal autumn-like weather conditions. After dropping the patient off, and then refueling, the trip back to Johnstown ended right at sunset, a perfect ending to a perfect day. This was the kind of day that even the crew lived for. I felt bad that their time with the Allouette was running out.

Louisville, Kentucky

IT WAS a cold and overcast November morning when I lifted the Allouette for the last time from the CVMH rooftop pad the aircraft now enroute to its new home in Louisville, Kentucky. The ship was packed with the required maintenance manuals, cans of transmission fluid, engine oil, tie downs and covers, my bags, few that they were, and the charts I needed for navigation.

I refueled in Wheeling, West Virginia, then in Cincinnati, arriving in Louisville close to five in the afternoon. Humana Hospital was within spitting distance of the Louisville airport (a UPS hub airport), so to expedite my departure for Dothan, Alabama, to visit my wife and daughters, the pilot on duty bunny-hopped me in the Allouette directly from the hospital, plopping me in front of the terminal where I caught my first flight toward home.

The airline flight allowed me to reflect on what I had done leaving my secure job at Rucker as a contract flight instructor dishing out instrument flight instruction to army student pilots. I had no permanent home with Rocky, not yet anyway. I wondered where I would end up, relieved of my relief-pilot duties. My wife and I had been on the outs for the past couple of years and I wasn't at all certain that we should be together. Ex-army helicopter pilots it seems are notorious vagabonds, difficult to stay married, difficult to offer hope of anything permanent where everyone was happy. I knew of one pilot who was on his third marriage — to the same woman. Maybe three times really is a charm. I felt my wife and I got married too young. She was twenty and I was twenty-five. Plus, I had certain notions of married life that didn't coincide with hers. Even our parents knew we were a mismatch. The Vietnam war had soured me toward all tradition, and my wife was an Italian Catholic enveloped in tradition. But I didn't want to be apart from my two daughters. Thus, I couldn't wait for a permanent position to open somewhere with the Rocky system so we could all be together again.

Flying out of Louisville lasted all of two months. I drove my 1974 Monte Carlo from Enterprise to Louisville for my first week of duty, a trip of about 540 miles. The lead pilot, a man of most unusual calm, allowed me to stay in the pilot quarters instead of spending money on a motel room. He was the night pilot and I was the day pilot. I had an army canvas cot I slept on, hospital food in the cafeteria which was pretty darn good, and I had a level of camaraderie with the medical crew that was the opposite to my experience in Johnstown. The crew was a paramedic and nurse combination, and there was a mixture of both male and female. I rotated seven days on and seven days off, drove home during my time off, and regretted each time I had to depart for Louisville. I felt no emotion from my wife, was saddened by our lack of harmony, and even more uncertain about our future together.

At Humana Hospital, the helicopter pad was on ground level in full view of the dispatch center and a short seventy-foot stroll from the pilot quarters. I spent practically every minute of my time (when I wasn't flying) seated next to the dispatcher on duty listening to area fire, police, and medical emergency calls on the scanner, ready to launch should a request for an air ambulance come through. Instead of waiting on pins and needles for a flight to surprise me out of the blue, I became aware of the potential for a flight much sooner than otherwise. I had had only one aborted flight with a patient onboard due to weather, out of Somerset, Pennsylvania, on my way to Pittsburgh, and was faced with a request for a hospital transfer from Salem, Indiana, to Louisville with a strong potential for snow showers enroute back. The skies in the Midwest during December always looked like snow could happen most anytime. This time the forecast was very favorable for light snow flurries. I decided to try the flight thinking I could always abort enroute to Salem.

At the Salem hospital, it took the crew longer to package the patient than normal, thus when I lifted the flurries had already started, and were getting worse. I hated to return the patient to the hospital in Salem but light snow flurries had morphed into thick flurries. The crew was strictly okay with my decision.

Springfield, Missouri

IT WAS early January 1989 when I learned Rocky was hiring four pilots for a new contract in Springfield, Missouri, at Cox Medical Center South. But to get the position, I had to interview with members of the hospital administration. Their previous vendor was Air Evac based out of West Plains, Missouri. The contract with them was nullified when one of their pilots crashed near a farmhouse after he took off in foggy weather. When the pilot wisely decided to abort, he made his approach to what appeared as level ground. Instead it was a row of rolled bales of hay. The pilot literally set the landing gear on top of a bale and the helicopter literally rolled off. Injuries were minor but the helicopter, a Bell 206 Jet Ranger, was destroyed.

Four pilots met in a room in the hospital and answered several questions pertaining to the weather, and the decision to go or not go based on the weather. One of the pilots had worked for Air Evac and told of how management pushed their pilots to take any and all flights almost despite the weather. The other two pilots were a husband and wife team with four sons. I was asked if I could work with a female pilot as a team member. I explained that as an instrument instructor I had dealt with several female army student pilots and saw no reason to think I couldn't be okay with a woman pilot on the contract. Our salary was $30,000 per year. It turned out the lead pilot, the one who had worked for Air Evac, was a warrant officer in the Missouri Army National Guard and an ex-police officer. He was also an inveterate chain smoker. Despite a no-smoking policy anywhere in the hospital and on hospital grounds, he acted totally oblivious to the rule. The pilot office and sleeping quarters were saturated with the rank smell of stale cigarette smoke. I did manage to get him to stop smoking in the sleeping room.

The hospital bought an MBB BO 105 CBS-4 helicopter which hadn't yet been delivered. To start the program, Rocky supplied the hospital with an AS 355F, a twin-engine helicopter that proved to be a nightmare to land without an occasional violent jolt to neck and back. Like the Allouette, the Twinstar's rotor system turned counterclockwise. It wasn't until I qualified later in the single-engine AStar that I learned the technique for landing and taking off without looking like a total fool. The technique, once learned, is so simple. In the Huey helicopter, to lift to a hover straight up I added generous left rear cyclic input; in the Twinstar I had to add generous right rear cyclic.

Rocky sent a company check airman from Billings, Montana, to get us up to speed in the aircraft. I flew first. An hour and a half later, he signed me off, checked out in a twin-engine helicopter. It was a matter of starting two engines instead of one, and should one of the engines fail, the preferred technique was a running landing, while trying not to overtax the other engine. It seemed insane, considering the army's method for pilot indoctrination and training. The other pilots also qualified after the same amount of flight time. A week later, I was on night duty. The smoker, being the lead pilot, opted to fly days for the first seven days so that he could deal with contract matters during daytime when hospital administrators were also at work. The husband and wife pair would then fly opposite each other day and night for a week, at which the normal rotation began.

I was very familiar with the Springfield area and surrounding communities from the ground. Flying, however, was another matter, especially reacting to a flight request. In those days, new pilot orientation was almost a matter of rolling the dice. Rocky Mountain Helicopters hired professional pilots, not babies, not like the army when a pilot became a pilot. Before a new-born army aviator was let loose, he had to operate with a more experienced pilot to learn proven techniques. In those days in the civilian EMS world, there was no such thing as two pilots flying together per aircraft to learn the ropes. That would have been too costly. Night vision goggles and autopilot would have been a much better option—also very expensive. Besides, the BK-117 was the only EMS helicopter in service (that I can recall) that could accommodate two pilots, three medical crew members (if one was in training), and two patients. The BK-117 was a beast.

During my time at Cox South, the very first time I flew to Kansas City was at night, the first time to St. Louis was at night, to Little Rock, Arkansas, was at night, to Columbia, Missouri, was at night. In fact, to every large city I ever had to fly to, at all the contracts I ever worked (except going to Pittsburgh), the first time was at night. Big cities have lots of lights. To find a hospital among all those lights was a nerve-wracking challenge. And the weather—what was it like enroute? So many concerns fraught with peril. In fact, on one flight from Springfield to St. Louis, I had to abort due to weather, landing at the Fort Leonardwood hospital pad, where I spent the remainder of the night. The medical crew continued patient transport by ground ambulance.

It turned out that most of the flights generated by the Springfield contract were scene flights, reacting either to a highway accident or to a local hospital in the aftermath of an accident. I relate three of my most notable patient flights, the imprint of the details still etched firmly in my mind.

It was two in the morning, the temperature in the single digits. By now Cox South had acquired its MBB BO 105 helicopter and all pilots were checked out. The nose of the aircraft, where my feet worked the anti-torque pedals, was cold, the ship's heated air never reaching down to warm them. The trip was to a small hospital seventy miles north of Springfield. The eighteen-year-old patient had been drag-racing, he hit a patch of ice, the car flipped, he was ejected. Upon arrival at the hospital, I helped the crew carry stretcher and equipment into the little ER, and where I would normally go back and wait at the helicopter, I instead remained in the ER to stay warm. I was in a room that had two large windows, one window viewed the ER staff and medical crew working on the patient. To my right was another large window that viewed the waiting room, where sat the young man's parents in obvious distress. The parents were not able to see what I could see in the ER. After several minutes, the ER doctor left the patient and went to the parents. I couldn't hear what he told them, but I saw the mother breakdown sobbing. The doctor went back into the ER, he and the staff and crew continued working on the young man. Then I saw them cease all attempts to revive him. I could hear through the open door of the room within which I sat the doctor declare the time of death. The doctor then left the room, went to the waiting room, and I watched him break the sad news. By now I was warm to the point of being uncomfortably hot. My chest had expanded with such a feeling of sorrow for the parents that I no longer wanted to watch the drama play out. I watched anyway. The doctor then led the parents into the emergency room. My eyes grew wide when I saw the mother struggle to get on top of the gurney. She straddled her son and began pounding his chest with her fists, yelling: "Wake up, Frankie! Wake up! Wake up! Frankie, wake up!" It was then that I left the room, went to the helicopter, and pondered in cold silence what I had just witnessed. The trip back to Springfield was a blur. And my feet felt like frigid blocks of ice as I refueled the aircraft.

I believe the worst job at any major hospital is that of chaplain, the person who gives spiritual comfort to the next of kin. Their calm fortitude to deal with such pain and suffering of parents and relatives had to be beyond anything I could imagine.

Bolivar is a small town thirty miles north of Springfield. It was summer, hot and humid as usual, sweaty muggy hazy. It was always a relief to get in the air, even if some tragedy was the reason for launching.

The landing zone was near a water tower close to the center of town. On approach, I saw ambulances, firetrucks, police vehicles, and dozens and dozens of onlookers all focused on the drama that had unfolded in this little town where hardly anything ever happens.

In the hot mugginess, a maintenance crew had been painting the town's water tower. Below were two helpers who sent up by rope whatever was needed. A steel ladder twenty feet long and about one foot wide had been attached to the rope and one of the men on top had been hauling it up when the rope slipped from his hands. The ladder fell straight down and imbedded in the head of one of the workers on the ground. The medical crew went to the ambulance where the victim was located. Firefighters, along with a local welder, had used an acetylene torch to remove the bulk of the ladder so that patient, and what was left of the ladder still imbedded in the young man's head, could fit inside the ambulance. The first rung of the ladder had made a deep imprint in the top of his skull, while the very bottom of one of the ladder's vertical rails had penetrated the top of the man's head and was sticking out through the bottom of his jaw. The other vertical rail missed the other side of his head completely.

The patient was loaded, his head covered by a bedsheet. I couldn't believe he was still alive. The trip back was frantic. The crew kept asking how much longer before we reached the hospital. I told them, "I'm pedaling as fast as I can!"

The fifteen-minute trip seemed to last forever. I pulled in as much power as I dared. But the BO 105 just slugged along, impervious to our laments—impervious to the trials of the human condition. Prior to landing, the crew began CPR. The young man's head was now in full view. We still had about two minutes to go. Throughout the final approach, I could see out of the corner of my left eye this man's devastating injury. How was he going to survive? What kind of life would he have? I didn't dwell. I brought the 105 to a high hover then settled gently onto the landing pad. The crew didn't need an expedited jarring touchdown to make matters worse.

The hospital ER staff that came out to assist stared wide-eyed at the condition of the patient for a split second before they and the crew unloaded him and wheeled him into the ER. I shut down and refueled. Afterward, I went to the ER, got a cup of coffee, then went outside sipping the hot liquid to calm my nerves. I was standing inside the entrance to the hospital when several people, a man, a woman, a teenage boy and girl, and a toddler were ushered by one of the chaplains into a comforting room outside the ER entrance. I knew immediately why they were there. The grief in their eyes said it all. I heard a muffled scream and then I left quickly for the pilot quarters.

The entire flight from start to finish stayed in my mind for days, for weeks. It was difficult not to think about it. I had seen bad injuries and wounds in Vietnam but not like this. Cox South had even set up counseling services for all first responders involved in the incident. By then it was one of many such episodes that I had witnessed, maybe none as dramatic, but even memories of lesser occurrences remain still.

The terrain that dominates southwest Missouri near Tablerock Lake is hilly, the roads winding and narrow, often without shoulders. The day was fresh and dry and cool with the first hint of fall. It was about three in the afternoon when we got the call, a head-on collision between a short-bed 1/2-ton pickup with three male occupants and an older model Oldsmobile. First responders had set the LZ in the middle of an intersection close to where the accident had occurred. Off to the side of the pickup was a body covered by a bedsheet. The ambulance crew was working on one of the men in the truck. I could see in the car a person slumped over the steering wheel (a young girl in her teens I later discovered). Sirens and any helicopter activity in these surrounding hills always draw a crowd. I had kept the helicopter running in anticipation of a quick loading. As I sat at the controls, a scratched and dented older model car drove up, stopped, a woman got out, ran first to the person covered by the bedsheet, then to the driver's side of the Oldsmobile, a car she must have recognized. The sound of the two idling engines behind me muted her screams. Several first responders rushed to her side. She tore away from them, and then three bystanders came and grabbed her and took her off to the side of the road, where I saw her break into hysterical sobs. The crew loaded the only survivor of the crash, I brought the engines up to rpm, and we took off.

It doesn't end there. The girl, a thirteen-year-old, had been given the keys to her parents' car (by her parents) with the chore of driving to the nearest convenience store for a carton of cigarettes. She must have been driving quite fast, according to the way the two vehicles looked. The pickup's front end was jammed into the cab, the heavier Oldsmobile had a shattered windshield and a young girl's head trapped between the steering wheel and the dash. The mother and father had first heard the sirens, then saw the helicopter sometime later, which prompted them to get in their other car to see what all the commotion was about. They had come on the scene directly after I had landed the BO 105 and the crew had exited with the stretcher and their equipment. I was later told, too, that the day after the accident the parents had visited Cox South hospital and asked if maybe the flight crew had found the carton of cigarettes and taken them, and if they had would they please give the carton back. I listened to this unbelievable account with a mixture of bemusement, bewilderment, and disbelief.

It wasn't often that we had a hospital transfer longer than a hundred and fifty miles. When a request came to take a man to a hospital in Paducah, Kentucky, to be closer to his family, who was I to think twice about taking a five-hundred-mile round trip, especially on a pretty day. We would have to refuel twice, going and returning. During any refueling the patient is to be taken out of the aircraft, which we did in Poplar Bluff, on our way to Paducah. Flights like these were pure pleasure. The patient was stable, the weather was clear, there was no panic. I likened reacting to a flight request, a highway accident for example, as going from zero to ninety in 4.5. For those who were adrenalin junkies as most of the medical crew were, they couldn't wait for a call. They often said they were in the mood for a good head trauma, or a gunshot, or a possible amputation, some dreadful violence to the human body upon which to test their medical skills. A person was identified by their injury or disorder. Heart patient transfers were boring. When they weren't charting directly after a flight, they were helping in the ER doing mundane chores. Of course, they wanted to fly. It was a prestigious job. One night, a call came in, I checked the weather, and declined the flight. The paramedic on duty looked outside, saw nothing but clear sky. He called and asked what the problem was. I said there was a good potential for fog. The temperature-dewpoint spread was one degree, the humidity at 98 percent. I could tell in his voice he was disappointed. Fifteen minutes later the fog was so dense I couldn't see across the street. He called and thanked me. He was one of my more favored medical crewmembers, someone who let me do my job of evaluating the weather the way only a pilot can do, especially when faced with the idea of losing visual contact with the ground at night. Others were okay with my piloting weather decisions, while a few still hesitated to trust me.

Hospitals that have a helicopter obviously wish to boost revenue. Typically, money is made, not because a helicopter was used, but because of the level of expensive care received in the hospital *after* the helicopter was used. It is a great PR tool, a symbol of high-quality care in competition with those hospitals that don't have a flight program. St. Johns Mercy Hospital just up the street had had a long-established flight program. They too had a BO 105 but a much older model. Gratefully, the two hospitals didn't hate each other like some did that were in the same city, each with a flight program. Competition was so fierce that CEOs were known to call each other unprintable names.

It was after my divorce that I became involved with a young female ER nurse whose ambition was to be a member of the flight team. She was very vocal about it which caused the flight crew to dismiss her desires out of hand. I knew her skills as a nurse to be far and above those of the flight crew. Jealousy among nurses and paramedics was epidemic. I thought politicians ate each other alive; medical professionals were far worse, sometimes to the detriment of the patient. My involvement with this young woman eventually costed me my job. Pilots are dispensable; not so nurses and paramedics. It's a wonder I hadn't been booted from the hospital in Johnstown, the nurses there so aggravated with my lack of jovial camaraderie. Jeff Lewis, the man who hired me, had made the comment one day that it's too bad pilots can't be neutered before reporting to a contract, there would be a lot less shuffling of skilled pilots from hospital to hospital. I had seen this at Allegheny General in Pittsburgh. A beautiful flight nurse had the squirms for a very handsome and very married pilot. I observed her all over him like hot butter on those occasions when I flew into Pittsburgh. However, the downside for a pilot to become involved with a female flight nurse was that if the pilot after a fashion rebuffed her continuing advances, he suddenly became unfit for duty as a pilot. Misery loves company, "I'll make him suffer, too," and it wouldn't be long before the lost-loved pilot is mysteriously gone.

I broke the news to my ex-wife who had to hear me say, "I've been fired …" three times before it finally registered. I was forking over $860 a month in child support. Now where was the money going to come from?

To make this unfortunate turn of events brief, I left the area, went to the Pacific Northwest, my tail tucked between my legs, and pretended to look for another flying job. I was too embarrassed to even try. I went to work for J.B. Hunt as a truck driver for six months, quit, then got a warehouse job at the Target Distribution Center in Pueblo, Colorado, two jobs I wouldn't wish on my worst enemy. My parents took me in so that I could make child support payments without the burden of paying rent or living alone. To go from flying to truck driving and warehouse work was such a blow to my ego that for six years I dreamt almost non-stop about flying again only to wake to a truth I couldn't seem to accept — that I had no flying job and was unlikely to fly again, that my reputation was so sullied that no one would ever hire me.

I did take advantage of the situation. I finished working on my Vietnam war novel, "The Sky Soldiers." I started college with the intent of teaching math and science. I spent two semesters in Juneau, Alaska, at the university. When I arrived back in the lower forty-eight in May 2000, my ex-wife told me that she still needed me to make child support payments to get my youngest daughter through college, beyond the original agreement. (By then I was using student loan money to make support payments.) I interviewed with Swift trucking company. Then decided to apply at Rocky. I had to convince my interviewer that I held no ill feelings toward Rocky Mountain Helicopters for terminating me. I really didn't. I figured I'd made my bed and had to sleep in it. (Actually, it was the hospital that fired me.)

St. Joseph, Missouri

I HAD a choice of working either in St. Joseph, Missouri, or Chanute, Kansas. I picked St. Joseph because it was close to where my oldest daughter was living and working in Kansas City, after she had graduated from college. I went through the Part 135 training in Olathe, Kansas, and was checked out in the AS 350 AStar. St. Joseph, Missouri, in the winter, was deceiving. What appeared as slashing and blowing rain was more like blowing ice-rain. Missouri weather was always treacherous: violent thunderstorms, tornadoes, ice storms, and occasionally blowing and drifting snow. I found a little apartment over a garage in Wathena, Kansas, near the St. Joseph Rosecrans Memorial Airport. The lead pilot had once been a flight paramedic, then decided to go to helicopter school, got his commercial rating, his instrument ticket, did a fair amount of instructing to increase his hours, and of all things, was hired by Rocky to be the lead pilot. However, he was not favored by either the chief flight nurse or the lead flight paramedic. He tended to turn down flights for weather even when the weather was way above Rocky's minimums, explaining to the crew that the forecast wasn't favorable. True or not, the perception of the crew was that he was chicken. He probably was in way over his head.

St. Joseph, Missouri, as a base location fifty miles north of Kansas City, offered aeromedical services to four states: Missouri, Kansas, Nebraska, and Iowa. The problem with this had to do with similar sounding names of towns in each of the states, or even in the same state. There was Maryville, Mayville, Maysville, and the town of Mary, as well as Independence, Missouri, and Independence, Kansas. Independence, Missouri, is a suburb of Kansas City, Missouri, and Independence, Kansas, is a little town in the south of Kansas near Coffeyville, just north of the Oklahoma state line. One day I got a scene call to go to a location east of Independence. My first thought was Independence, Missouri, since that was closest to St. Joseph. Once in the air, I asked for coordinates. I plugged them into the GPS which indicated the scene location was some 200 miles away—far, far to the south. I quizzed the dispatcher. When he realized his mistake, sending the wrong helicopter and crew, it was then that I realized that I had to be more inquisitive when sent anywhere on a scene call. In the heat of "battle" even the dispatcher can be as flustered as the first responders, trying to do the right thing for victims of an accident. It was the Chanute, Kansas, helicopter that should have been called to go to the scene just east of Independence, Kansas. Not me!

I became privy to another issue involving latitude and longitude coordinates. Those first responders with a handheld GPS may relay the correct set of coordinates but in a format other than how I programmed the aircraft GPS. In other words, the dispatcher had to know for certain which format was being used. And even the dispatcher didn't quite understand the nuances of the different formats. More than once I plugged into the aircraft GPS the numbers given me, written down by either the nurse or paramedic, only to learn something was wildly askew. Since I brought this subject up, I shall attempt to clarify this issue about the three different lat/long formats.

Latitude/Longitude Formats

THE THREE different formats are:

1. **Degrees, minutes, seconds.** Example: North (latitude) 36 degrees, 15 minutes, and 30 seconds by West (longitude) 79 degrees, 30 minutes, and 45 seconds equates to N 36° 15′ 30″ by W 79° 30′ 45″.
2. **Degrees, minutes decimal seconds.** Example: North 36 degrees, 15 minutes decimal 50 by West 79 degrees, 30 minutes decimal 75 equates to N 36° 15.5′ by W 79° 30.75′.

3. **Degrees decimal minutes & seconds.** Example: N 36 degrees decimal 258 by W 79 degrees decimal 513. (N 36.258° by W 79.513°) (15′ 30″ = 15.5′ = .258 and 30′ 45″ = 30.75′ = .513)

To start we have N 36° 15′ 30″ (the first format scheme). To convert 30″ to its decimal equivalent, divide 30″ by 60 (60 seconds per minute) to equal .5, we now get N 36° 15.5′. Next we have W 79° 30′ 45″. To convert 45″ to its decimal equivalent, divide 45″ by 60 to equal .75, we now get W 79° 30.75′. Both sets of coordinates are now in the second format scheme of degrees, minutes decimal seconds. To get to the third format scheme of degrees decimal minutes & seconds, do this: divide 15.5′ by 60 (60 minutes per degree) to equal .258 and divide 30.75′ by 60 to equal .513. Both sets of coordinates are now in the third format scheme: N 36.258° by W 79.513°.

As I recall, the aircraft GPS used the degrees, minutes decimal seconds format, #2 above. On public relations (PR) flights to the outlying EMS community, this is the time to introduce formatting issues. Hopefully, it helps more than confuses.

I have an iPhone. I am located at the following coordinates: N 37° 57′ 23″ by W 104° 48′ 17″. With both changed into the degrees, minutes decimal seconds format, I come up with: N 37° 57.38′ by W 104° 48.28′. Changed into degrees decimal minutes & seconds format, I get: N 37.956° by W 104.805°.

The main thing to remember is that in the heat of trying to do the right thing, there has got to be time to slow down long enough — *to do the right thing.* I doubt that any first responder with a handheld GPS is even going to know, when questioned, the format he's got programmed in his GPS. The very way a set of lat/long coordinates is said over the radio is basically key. If read aloud correctly, in the heat of chaos, the dispatcher should catch the format nuance.

In fact, the dispatcher should be made aware of what the GPS format scheme is and tutored on the various formats and how confusion can reign if the right lat/long format is not spoken to the pilot.

One other tidbit I learned. Enroute to a scene, particularly during the day, I always asked those on the ground to let me know when they could either hear me or see me. If they could at least hear the aircraft, I knew I was close. When they reported they had a visual, I asked that they steer me toward them if I wasn't already on a direct course. Sometimes a scene isn't on a highway at all, but in some remote location hidden by trees or some other obstruction.

Joplin, Missouri

ON MY time off I performed relief-pilot duties at the contract in Kansas, flying out of the Chanute airport. After several visits there, I got to know and like the medical crew and the other three pilots, all who wanted me to join their merry band. It wasn't until the helicopter and crew were pulled from Chanute and sent to Joplin, Missouri, that I decided to transfer. Freeman Hospital in Joplin was in direct competition with St. Johns of Joplin, where the CEOs, like I mentioned, hated each other. St. Johns' helicopter was a BK-117. The St. Johns' CEO proclaimed to the surrounding ambulance community that because the BK was a twin-engine machine, their helicopter was much safer, despite the reputation of the AS 350 as a very reliable, single-engine, EMS helicopter. Maybe the 117 was safer in that regard but I never thought their pilots were very conservative when it came to the weather. They launched repeatedly in crap I wouldn't stick my big toe in. Years later, during the 2011 Joplin tornado that ripped from west to east across the middle of the city, killing outright 158 people, I learned that their helicopter had been completely destroyed, just as the St. Johns' eight-story hospital building had been torqued by the EF-5 twister on its foundation some eighteen degrees, requiring the hospital to be rebuilt at another location in the city. The on-duty pilot had failed to move the helicopter to their hangar at the Joplin airport, while the Freeman pilot had moved their AS 355 N model Twinstar to their secure location at the same airport. (This was several years after I had left Joplin for Florida, and other contract locations.)

I became the lead pilot at Joplin, and performed in this capacity for three years. During that time Air Methods out of Denver bought up Rocky and all its contracts, becoming now the largest purveyor of EMS helicopters, pilots, and mechanics in the United States. Because Air Methods vended for St. Johns, they couldn't vend at Freeman Hospital which would have been a conflict of interest. Ballard Aviation out of Wichita came into the picture and took over. The entire Freeman flight crew went to work for them. Nothing changed except that our AS 350 B2 was replaced by an AS 355 N model Twinstar. Of all the aircraft I'd flown, I liked the B2 best, it was such a powerful, sporty little job. The Twinstar, heavier than the B2, had to be dragged into the air, like lifting a ball and chain. The AS 350 B2, nicknamed Écureuil (squirrel), sprinted upward as if jerked by some unseen hand.

In Joplin I met my second wife through a dating service. Her little two-bedroom house was a block from the hospital. She worked as an office-manager and bookkeeper for a Mexican fast food chain exclusive to Joplin. She wasn't happy with her work, mainly because of the boss, and started looking on the Internet for a pet boutique and bakery business to buy, preferably in Florida. She hated the icy winters in southwest Missouri, bound and determined not to live the rest of her life in freezing boredom. She had ambitions to be her own boss.

Her desire to move prompted me to interview with Metro Aviation headquartered in Shreveport, Louisiana, after she found the perfect business to buy in Destin. They had a pilot opening in Marianna, Florida. The Marianna location had a sister base in Santa Rosa not far from Destin. On the day of my interview the chief pilot casually mentioned that the dispatch center hadn't heard from the Santa Rosa crew. It was eight in the morning. Fifteen minutes later he informed me that aircraft and crew were officially declared missing. An hour later he got word that the ship, an MBB BO 105, was found in the Choctawhatchee Bay north of the Santa Rosa base. There were three fatalities. And it had been an aborted night flight due to weather.

Destin, Florida

NOW I had the choice of being at either the Marianna base or Santa Rosa. I picked Santa Rosa because it was closer to Destin and the pet boutique. My wife and I couldn't afford the homes in Destin, so we found a small three-bedroom, two-bath house in Mary Esther, a tiny suburb of Fort Walton Beach, in the Eglin AFB and Valparaiso area.

My wife and I had already had one vacation together, in Mexico, at Playa del Carmen south of Cancun. Prior to packing up all our household furniture and belongings we vacationed one more time in Playa del Carmen in late October 2004. We moved into our little Mary Esther house on December 15, 2004, thinking this would be our last move, that the Florida panhandle would be our forever home. Never say never. The pet boutique and bakery business barely made enough profit to think long range. I didn't care for flying so close to the coast, coastal weather being such that clouds and visibility were suitable for flight one minute not so great the next. It was a nightmare to predict decent weather at night. The hurricane season of 2005, of New Orleans and Katrina fame, soured me completely to the area despite the sugar white beaches and the blue and aqua blue Gulf waters.

Having spent so many duty hours as a "flight for life" pilot, I came to realize the human condition, that life turns on a dime. One minute all is right with the world, the next minute tragedy. Both the Santa Rosa aircraft and the Marianna aircraft were called to the same highway accident on Interstate 10. It was a rollover caused by a woman allowing her van's right-side wheels to leave the edge of the highway. In her attempt to right the situation the van flipped several times. With her were three of her children, two young boys and a young girl. Following close behind to see it happen was her husband and another child in their second car.

The Marianna aircraft had landed ahead of me, and was loading the two young boys, while I waited for the mother and daughter to be packaged for transport. I knew the boys were in worst shape. The mother was hysterical wondering about her sons; the daughter was weeping silently. The pilot in the other aircraft spoke to me over the radio: "I think one of the boys is a goner. How are your patients fairing?"

"I think the mother is out of her mind with worry."

"She'll be more so when she gets to the hospital. I pity her."

I had learned about the husband while waiting to liftoff. The image of the accident, I knew would be with him for the rest of his life, his family almost decimated in the briefest instant of time. It had been that way for me ever since I began this job. Launching at a moment's notice to pure despair. I remember an accident south of Springfield, at night, a pickup truck in a head-on collision. One of the firefighters didn't realize that the person he was helping to extract from the vehicle with the jaws-of-life was his brother, the brother was so unrecognizable. It was a fear all EMS workers had, that of coming upon a loved one at the scene of a horrific accident. It almost happened to me, when a call came to go to an accident site not far from where I and my family lived in Nixa, a little bedroom community just south of Springfield. As I flew over the road where the accident had occurred, I could see below that neither vehicle was one my wife would have been driving.

Prior to the hurricane season of 2005, some distance from shore were undersea sandbars. Hurricane Dennis, making landfall as a category three, managed to erase these sandbars which were like a barrier to sharks to keep them from migrating close to the beaches. Now the sharks were routinely feeding nearer to the coastline. It was a bright beautiful sunny day, not a single cloud anywhere, not even floaters in the distance, the Gulf waters a sparkling blue, the white sandy beaches dazzling in mid-morning light. The call announced a shark attack.

We launched and while enroute to Sandestin from Santa Rosa, the dispatcher asked me to patrol the waters offshore to look for sharks. I said I would and then wondered why the diversion from going directly to the LZ where the ground ambulance was parked. The crew got on the radio and asked. The victim was deceased, her body drained of blood. She was a fourteen-year-old girl brought in by two rescuers who saw the attack. I landed in a parking lot near the ambulance. I kept the B0 105 running. The crew got out and went to the ambulance and was inside for about ten minutes when I saw them get out and come back to the aircraft. "We got some great photos. We'll have to show them to you." "Pictures? Of what?" "The girl. Her right thigh looks like a gnawed-on chicken bone."

I brought the two engines up to full rpm. It was all I could do not to visualize what they must have taken pictures of—a denuded teenage girl, drained of blood, mangled, probably pasty white. Later I got to thinking about such an attack. I had in mind that she was curly-haired, had a diminutive figure, cute as a bug, bright-eyed, full of life. But not anymore. I remember reading about a man who had been attacked by a bear in Alaska. He described the munching crunching sounds as the bear gnawed on him, his scalp being ripped, his bones penetrated by claws and teeth. It was a completely visceral experience devoid of thought, just sensation, pain without contemplation — like *how is this going to end?* A moment like that must be when death is a blessing — the ultimate escape. What went through the girl's mind when she first realized she was in dreadful danger? The first time I met face to face with my third (and current) wife I posed that question. She gave a most fascinating and lucid answer: the young girl's guides (angels) probably pulled her conscious-ness out of her body before (or at least directly after) the shark began its frenzy so she wouldn't experience the emotional trauma of the attack. My wife had had a serious fall from a horse. She doesn't remember her head hitting the hard gravel road, claiming likewise that her angels *yanked* her *during* the fall. She spent nine days in the hospital after a craniotomy to drain two hematomas. Though she was awake, she remembered nothing. It was as near to an NDE (near death experience) as she had ever had.

I never did look at the photos of the teenage girl. I refused. The medical crew I'm certain used the pictures for edification (education) purposes.

From then on whenever I flew a patient to Pensacola, on the return to base I low leveled just far enough from shore to spot any evidence of close-in sharks. Past Destin, and Sandestin, going east, there is an isolated public beach called Topsail Hill Preserve State Park quite apart from those beaches near the big hotels. The first flight over the water out from the beach I spied an estimated 50 sharks. The next flight over the same area netted 80 to 90. The last estimate was close to 150 tiger sharks. I reported these sightings to the local authorities, thinking that the biology department of one of the Florida universities would want to investigate this phe-nomenon. I never did find out if any Florida university did an investigation.

The program director of the two Florida bases was a balding, pudgy-fingered man who drove a Mercedes, had a scanner radio to listen to all area police and fire calls, and who monitored the calls for air ambulance services. Anytime a request was declined, for whatever reason, he would first alert the lead pilot, then call pilot quarters to quiz the on-duty pilot why the decline. This put major pressure on us pilots. The director was your classic bean counter. When Metro Aviation finally got wind of his meddling, the company gave the hospital an ultimatum: "… either he's fired or we pull our two helicopters." The program director was let go.

Standard operating practice was that pilots were to report to their home com-pany anytime anyone questioned a GO-NOGO weather decision. To question was to (eventually) pressure a pilot to launch against his better judgment. During my tenure as lead pilot in Joplin, I continually reiterated to hospital administration that aviation companies had to comply with FAA mandates: about flight operations, crew rest, and prescribed maintenance procedures. We were an aviation entity first, sanctioned by the FAA, *then we take care of victims of accidents and patient transfers to higher-care facilities.* The same program director the day after the MBB BO 105 fatal accident, wanted Metro Aviation to supply the Santa Rosa base with an immediate replacement aircraft—no time to collect thoughts or even grieve the loss of three crewmembers. The director was a man without a heart.

The EMS helicopter industry had (and still does) its share of gung-ho pilots and medical crew. Whenever an EMS accident occurred there was a write-up to highlight how and why the accident happened. Food for thought. A common pattern was pushing the weather at night, losing visual contact with the ground, unable to control the aircraft—spatial disorientation a foregone conclusion. A few accidents occurred due to unfamiliarity with the aircraft, the topography of the area, even lack of fuel. I learned over time that of all the requests for air ambulance service about ten percent was for life threatening conditions where helicopter transport saved a life. The other ninety percent the patient could have gone by ground ambulance without undue harm or later difficulties for not having used the helicopter. Occasionally, when it was time for ground ambulance crew shift change, they would call the helicopter to take the patient rather than run into overtime. This didn't happen often, but often enough to know it was improper.

It's strange how a state like Florida with its six million population could be so dark down the middle at night. A trip to Gainesville one night proved scary, with low clouds unseen until wisps of strata raised my hackles. There were few residential or city lights visible, and when I got to my destination at five in the morning, I knew not to attempt a trip back to base until daylight. One of the crew was irritated that he would be late getting off duty. I didn't feel sorry for him. It amazed me that after the fatal accident the year before some of the crew still didn't realize the dangers of going into instrument meteorological conditions (IMC), especially at night.

Branson West, Missouri

MY WIFE was no longer enamored with Florida, or the pet boutique and bakery business, and wanted to return to southwest Missouri as soon as she could find a willing buyer. In May 2006, I left our home in Mary Esther and drove to Missouri where Metro could use me at their Branson West base, south of Springfield. One of their pilots had been called to active duty in Afghanistan and I was to fill in during his year of absence. Meantime, my wife would continue to run the business and occupy our home. The 2006 hurricane season promised, according to the weather people, to be worse than the 2005 Katrina season. It turned out to be a complete dud.

It was pure delight to be checked out in the Eurocopter EC 135 P2 model. A glass cockpit and flip a switch to start each engine. The tail rotor was a semi-enclosed, ten-bladed fan that made the ship wiggle like crazy during landing. My check airman was a pilot on the contract, a pleasant mannered person with lots of patience. He acquired his

Eurocopter EC 135 P2

helicopter training through the civilian world, had built his hours instructing, and then flying at one of the Branson helicopter tour companies. The day I took my check ride, he was being given an FAA checkout as a check airman. Three professional pilots in the same ship, one of them from the FAA there to help. There is a saying about a visit from the FAA: *we're not happy until you're not happy.* That would be true of any visit by any government agency. During my check ride, my trainer was forgetting to have me do one last maneuver: the fixed-pedal tail rotor emergency landing. Thus, I reminded him by pointing to my feet, at which time he got the message. I was ready to be cut loose and have the EC 135 all to myself.

I had finally come full circle. The EC 135 belonged to St. Johns' hospital in Springfield, Cox South's competition. Cox South's helicopter had become the MD

MD 902 Explorer

902 Explorer, a no tail rotor (NOTAR) aircraft, using airflow through the tail boom along with adjustable vanes to handle helicopter anti-torque issues. It was an aircraft that I would never have the privilege of flying. St. Johns, instead of operating exclusively out of Springfield, created three separate bases: one in Branson West, another in Bolivar (of steel-ladder-through-the-head fame), and the

third in St. Robert, Missouri, near Fort Leonardwood. Bolivar had the old MBB BO 105 aircraft and St. Robert had an EC 135 P1 model. The medical crew didn't know the full story why I was terminated at Cox South. Not knowing the details, I sensed their animosity toward me from day one. They didn't like, either, that I wasn't required to be babysat, as were pilots fresh to EMS flying and to the EC 135 aircraft. What for? I knew Springfield and the surrounding area like the back of my hand. I did not need to be coached on how to do a job I had been successful at for more than twelve years.

Meanwhile, my wife continued to run the store in Destin. I did my rotations at the Branson West base, and went to visit her about once a month for a week. Meantime, I stayed with my youngest daughter living in Nixa some 30 miles north of Branson West. Then I found a used Toyota motorhome, moved it to a campground near the base, and enjoyed campground life through the summer, into the fall, and during a cold winter. That winter an ice storm blanketed all of Springfield. Two days later I flew over the city that sparkled reflected sunlight from ice clinging to the branches of trees. Thankfully, the ice storm didn't get down to my little RV motorhome. Interstate 44 that runs from northeast to southwest, north of Springfield, seems the cut off between freezing rain and snow — snow north of I-44, freezing rain and ice south of I-44. How does Mother Nature know to do that?

By spring 2007 one of the Branson West pilots decided to jump ship and become a corporate pilot for a local entrepreneur. The pay was good, the hours would probably be lousy, and I cautioned him of being required to fly in all kinds of weather. Likely he wouldn't have the luxury of turning down a flight due to the weather. The lay person really doesn't have a sense of a pilot-in-command's responsibility as to the safe operation of an aircraft. They don't know that the FAA takes a dim view of any pilot who doesn't exercise his command-pilot prerogative.

Harlingen, Texas

I GAVE notice to the St. Johns' program director that I would like to fill the open position. The pilot in Afghanistan was due back home in May. I felt the Branson West location was the perfect place to be when my wife finally sold the Florida business and the house, and moved back to Joplin. But the medical crew nixed the idea. They didn't want me. Instead, they opted to hire a young, low-time pilot (age 29) barely wet behind the ears. I had to find a new home with Metro. I picked Harlingen, Texas, eight miles north of the U.S.-Mexico border, not far from Brownsville. The base was hard pressed to keep pilots, there being other more favorable locations to hang one's pilot shingle. Somehow, I knew this would be my last EMS base.

I visited my wife in Florida as before and finally went there for the sale of the store. Now to sell the house. Her two sons came and helped pack up our belongings. They then drove their mother lock, stock, and barrel to Joplin. Her youngest son lived rent-free in a large, one-hundred-year-old farmhouse owned by a doctor and his wife, their own massive home on the same property but hidden from the farmhouse. The understanding was that my wife's son would help the doctor do chores around the property. A win-win situation. My wife found space in the farmhouse for all our furniture and stuff and settled in. To me the farmhouse represented peace and calm after my years as a pilot. I wanted desperately to relax, to kick back, drink beer, and while away the last of my days not in a constant state of panic. Ever since I joined the army back when I was eighteen, I had never had a regular circadian rhythm. Nights, days, mornings, evening twilight, all were a jumble. I never spent a night without dreaming, odd nonsensical dreams. I worked harder in my sleep than during my waking hours.

Our "empty-house" payments were fourteen hundred dollars a month. I had to keep this job in Harlingen. By the time the house was sold, during the 2008 housing downturn, it had been unoccupied for seven months.

The helicopter at the Harlingen base was an AS 350 B2, my favorite. The medical crew was mostly Hispanic. They respected me and my judgment and I in turn respected them. My relationship with these guys was the best I'd ever had with any medical crew.

Nine years before my arrival in south Texas, the contract had had an accident where all three crewmembers died. The Rio Grande valley sports numerous small towns from west of McAllen to Brownsville and the Gulf coast. South of the border are Matamoros and Reynosa with thousands of residents. The whole valley was well lit. But north of the valley it was dark, pitch dark, and thankfully flat. The crew back then reacted to a scene call that took them well away from all ground reference lights. The pilot developed spatial disorientation and put the helicopter into the ground. It was decided that using night vision goggles should be the norm. While I didn't care to be checked out in their use while I was on army active duty, I welcomed them now—mainly because I had no choice. I was amazed at how well I could see. Night became day, or so it seemed. Before my NVG training, I had become very familiar with the lights of the entire Rio Grande valley. But with the goggles on, the lights became a mass of brightness where it was difficult to distinguish the location of what I knew and where I knew it to be. The pilot could flip the whole ensemble from right in front of the eyes up and out of the way, easier now to distinguish the location of places without all the added brightness. I took two trips to San Antonio at night and was grateful that I had them to wear.

I hadn't liked coastal weather in the Fort Walton Beach-Destin area. South Padre Island and the Gulf coast were a constant source of medical flights, from drownings to watercraft accidents. Visibility often went from clear to three miles or less in a heartbeat, like the coast of the Florida panhandle. Cloud coverage was also deceiving, difficult at night to steer clear of them much less remain below them by any amount of space. Mexicans that had illegally crossed the border were another source of patient flights, some who had been hiding in an abandoned shack or house and discovered near death, or chased by the border patrol while riding in a van packed with other illegals, the van crashing in the flat spaces north of the conglomeration of cities rendering some seriously injured, even killed. The scent of their unwashed bodies in the cramped space of the helicopter was a thing to behold.

My wife living in Joplin wanted to buy a little bar/grill that was within a mile of the farmhouse. The owner was asking $20,000 for the business. There was no building to purchase, just take over the tables and chairs and the equipment, and what there was left of the food in the refrigerators and freezers. It sounded too good to be true. We didn't have that kind of money, so I told her to offer him $6,000, the amount of last year's tax refund. The man grumbled but took the offer. When my wife gets focused, she has tunnel vision, nothing else is important. Our marriage wasn't so important as it had been in the beginning. The pet boutique and bakery in Florida proved that. I was glad to be rid of it and thought that once we were settled in Joplin that cozy harmony would return. It didn't. She needed a new focus. The bar/grill became it and I knew my second marriage was doomed.

I became the Harlingen base safety officer. I counseled the crew repeatedly that they had as much say in refusing a flight due to weather as the pilot. The lead pilot, ex-army, not a Vietnam veteran, but a twenty-year career man, called each request to fly a "mission." I tried to explain to him that a mission was a military term; a mission was an activity fraught with danger; a mission was different than an EMS flight request in the civilian world. A mission was something you might not return from, like you could be killed. A medical flight, on the other hand, was something you had better survive, completely unscathed, helicopter and all, otherwise you don't go.

Before I arrived, the lead pilot had had a flight at night. He was wearing the night vision goggles and felt that because he could see through the beginnings of fog it was alright to continue. Then the fog became denser, to the point where he knew he had to abort. He landed in an open field close to a barbwire fence. He had a lot of explaining to do. I don't think he learned anything from the experience. His cohort at the contract was a crop duster during the day, using a Bell G-47 helicopter, and was on EMS duty at night, no consideration for crew rest. This guy was a hotdog. The crew on occasion described some of his antics with the base B2 helicopter, like landing too close to railroad tracks and a moving train.

Wintertime. A fourth pilot showed up, a crop duster pilot, but one who used a Piper Pawnee. He had worked for Metro before in the Rio Grande valley. Now that the season was over it was time to fill in the fourth slot.

He wasn't goggle qualified. He was scheduled to go through training soon. February 5, 2008, he and the medical crew were lost when the aircraft entered a thin, low-lying layer of clouds over the lagoon off South Padre Island. (This accident was mentioned earlier.) I was visiting my wife at the farmhouse in Joplin when the mechanic called me at six in the morning and told me the aircraft had crashed. He said there were no survivors.

My whole being sank. As the story went, crew and pilot were reacting to a flight request on the Island. It was night, around 11 p.m. The pilot experienced a case of vertigo, the aircraft careened downward, the helicopter entered the water nose down. The paramedic was found minus his head. The pilot's face was gone. The male flight nurse was just simply dead. Because the pilot wasn't yet goggle qualified, he obviously wasn't wearing a set. The crew, however, was qualified and had theirs on. They tried to advise the pilot where to go because they could see just fine. It didn't help. It only confused.

I cut my time short with my wife. At the base, everyone was numb. No one knew what to say. A diving crew salvaged as much of the aircraft (and body parts) as they could. Then they started dredging personal belongings, aircraft chunks, bits and pieces of the instrument panel, bringing the findings to a hangar near the base. The mechanic and I sorted through the wreckage, handling credit cards, photos, a watch, a wedding band, flashlights, scissors, rolls of medical tape.

Everyone attended the memorial service, a service I will never forget because I constantly choked back tears. Had the pilot been NVG qualified, I was certain the accident wouldn't have happened. An accident like that is a lawyer's dream come true. The flight nurse had told his fiancé that she was to sue the hell out of everyone associated with the flight program if he was ever killed in a crash. This declaration was less than four days old when the crash occurred. It was said that the crew asked the pilot over the intercom (which must have gone out on the radio), "… is this the end?" The pilot replied, "Yes, this is the end." True or not, it was all too spooky.

The paramedic's wife and another woman, his mistress, attended the memorial service and funeral.

The pilot's family was there, his wife, teenage son and daughter. You could tell who was to blame for the accident. The pilot's family stood apart from everyone, not knowing what to say to the families of the deceased. I had known four flight instructors at Fort Rucker who had been killed during training. I had been associated with Rocky Mountain Helicopters, Ballard Aviation, Air Methods, and Metro Aviation during the aftermath of six fatal EMS accidents. I did some research once and learned that in recent years king crab fishing off the coast of Alaska, logging in the Pacific Northwest, and EMS helicopter flying were the three most dangerous occupations in the United States, the most preventable accidents being EMS helicopter flying. Both medical crew and pilot can say NOGO. Stop, cease, desist. When they don't it makes me wonder their commitment to their calling. Is it reasonable? Do they not understand that you can do the most good for the greatest number of people by not neglecting the odds? It takes a long time to gain public confidence after a fatal EMS flying accident.

The replacement aircraft for the Harlingen base was in Traverse City, Michigan. I was volunteered to go get it. I did not want to go, fearful something bad would happen. I caught a commercial flight out of Harlingen to Houston, changed planes to fly to Minneapolis, then another flight from Minneapolis to Traverse City. I arrived at midnight to temperatures in the teens. Harlingen's temperature was 85 degrees when I left. My winter clothing was a thin jacket, no hat or gloves, and sneakers. I rode the shuttle bus to the Holiday Inn Express motel with the flight crew that brought me to Traverse City. I looked forlorn, still reeling from the memorial and funeral services four days before. There was no way to grab a quick beer. Everything was closed.

That morning the mechanic drove me to the Traverse City base and I started checking out the AS 350 B model AStar I was to fly back. He was in the process of a complicated aircraft inspection. The mechanic promised he would be done by noon. By two o'clock he was still enmeshed in the inspection. At three o'clock the mechanic asked that I do an engine runup and leak check. I went through the other checks as well. I didn't like the way the hydraulics felt, an ever so slight, unidentifiable "hiccup" felt in the cyclic control stick. Of all the aircraft systems associated with the AStar, I thought the hydraulic system the weakest link. In fact, the hydraulic system was the cause of a fatal accident in Norfolk, Nebraska, when the pilot didn't realize he had not engaged the right button to turn the hydraulics back on after a system check. I told the mechanic about the errant check but he could find nothing wrong. Three times I did the check; three times I felt the hiccup. The mechanic shrugged and said he couldn't feel the slight momentary feedback I felt.

I finally got off at around five o'clock, certain that something dreadful was going to happen. It was a much later start than I wanted. This meant that wherever I spent the night, I would get there long after dark. I refueled in Kalamazoo, then called it quits in Lafayette, Indiana, home of Purdue University. I drove into town using an FBO courtesy car. The hotel was sponsoring a college event and everywhere in the lobby and in the halls were students all slicked and dressed in their finest. I had never seen so many lovely young women. I spent my time in the hotel bar slowly nursing one Blue Moon after another. After my limit of three, I called it quits. I had a long way to go to Harlingen.

The next day it was cloudy with a steady wind out of the southeast. My ground speed was a pathetic 70 knots. I wondered when the hydraulic system was going to rear its ugly head. I slugged my way to Jackson, Tennessee, where I had had enough fighting the wind, and my fears. I got another room for the night. A worker at the FBO had brought me into town, so I was without a car. There was no place close where I could get a beer. All through the night I couldn't sleep. What the hell was wrong with the hydraulic system? The little hiccup was there every time I made the check. Even though I was well trained to handle a hydraulic failure, I didn't want a real failure to *test that skill*!

Metro Aviation wanted the aircraft in Shreveport, for check ride purposes, so that's where I ended the first leg of the ferry-flight journey. The chief pilot quickly arranged a commercial flight for me to Springfield, Missouri, where my wife picked me up. It would be another week before I had to get a flight to Shreveport so I could take an annual check ride, and then get the aircraft to Harlingen. Each pilot had two check rides per year, one in their primary aircraft and another in the designated spare. The spare for Harlingen was the MBB BO 105, which meant that those not previously qualified would be in for a twin-engine treat. The rigid rotor head of the BO 105 was such that German test pilots were able to momentarily have the machine upside down, something not normally done in a helicopter. There was a video of a German test pilot who showed the aircraft's remarkable capabilities, a video not widely distributed for fear those not qualified would try the maneuver with a not so favorable outcome. It was nice to know that if a severe case of turbulence caused the 105 to become momentarily inverted that pilot and crew would or could survive. I recall a return flight from Columbia, Missouri, to Springfield where the turbulence triggered the crew to moan and complain that their stomachs didn't feel good and getting worse by the minute. I had to tell them to be quiet or I might succumb to feelings of nausea myself. You don't want a sick pilot, I told them. It was the rigid rotor system that made any flight in turbulence not a merry ride, for crew or pilot.

I took my check ride in the same AStar I flew in from Traverse City. It was during the first autorotation that the glitch with the hydraulic system became slightly more pronounced. I told the check airman about the strange feeling in the cyclic control stick and when he reduced the throttle and lowered the collective lever, for some reason he didn't sense the same feedback. That puzzled me. On my second practice autorotation the feedback was still there but I dismissed it as not *that* obvious. Directly after the check ride, I made tracks for Harlingen to get the ferry flight completed.

The Harlingen mechanic gave the aircraft a good once over and checked the logbooks. I told him about the hydraulic glitch but he said he wasn't going to investigate it unless I wrote it up. I took that as a challenge. *Write it up or shut up*. So, I wrote it up. Sure enough, after a more thorough inspection, he found a major mechanical issue in one of the components of the system. The aircraft I had flown all the way from Traverse City to Harlingen, had used on a check ride, all the while had a discrepancy that might have caused a significant hydraulic failure any time after leaving Traverse City. The death of the medical crew and pilot, this hydraulic glitch, the universe was trying to tell me something. Then in early May the almost impossible happened: the house in Mary Esther sold, but I had to fork over $6,000 in the process. The buyer got us for $7,500 less than what my wife and I paid.

Now I didn't need this flying job anymore. Now I could quit the stress and the rat race. Now I could go live with my wife.

The contract was short one pilot. I couldn't depart now or the Harlingen base would be short two pilots, and therefore be unable to operate 24/7. I told Metro that I wouldn't leave until they found my replacement. The chief pilot emailed me a proposal: We'll pay you $60,000 per year to stay (which was $10,000 more than I was making). Very tempting but the gods had spoken. It was time to get out.

It was the end of May and I had no idea when I'd make tracks for Missouri. I wasn't too sure, either, that my wife even wanted me. My last two visits had been weird. By the middle of June Metro had found my replacement. But it would take a week, maybe more, to get him trained and checked out. When he came aboard, I went on night duty so that he could work days to get familiar with the area before doing his first stretch of nights. He was required to have five local and/or long-distance area medical flights before any night duty. His first seven days on duty he netted zero flights. Thus, I remained on nights.

Two very expensive sets of night vision goggles had been lost in the crash. This meant there weren't enough goggles to fit a full crew of three people. I missed wearing them. (It didn't matter; the replacement aircraft wasn't configured for NVGs anyway.) When I had used them, fitting them to my helmet, then gazing up at the stars, the stars appeared as if looking through the Hubble space telescope, ten times the number than could be seen with the naked eye. I saw the blinking lights of aircraft flying toward San Antonio over a hundred miles away. In the interim, while on night duty, I netted ten scene flights. Though we pilots could sleep while on duty, at night I never slept — I was committed to keeping track of the weather. I didn't care for a patient transfer to San Antonio, too many nighttime booby traps — mainly the weather. Why do they wait for night to get a patient on its way to a larger hospital in a bigger city 200 miles away? Besides, when the helicopter was gone that long for a single patient it meant local critical scene calls were neglected.

Mentally, I was wearing down. That our house in Florida sold right before the official start of hurricane season was a minor miracle. The insurance industry had a way of withholding coverage once hurricane season was under way which meant that home buyers took a chance buying a house should a hurricane be looming on the horizon. I had fashioned plywood boards to fit all the windows. But I had to go to Mary Esther myself to put them up should a hurricane be imminent. With the house finally sold, I was now on the verge of calm. After 38 years a pilot, a rent-free farmhouse to live in, it all seemed a dream come true.

I had already driven my little Toyota motorhome to my mother's house in Pueblo. At the RV park where I had lived for over a year in Harlingen, management rented me this little 6x8 box that had a bed, a sink, a microwave oven, a TV, a bathroom and shower. It had no windows. A small window air conditioner was mounted right above the head board of the bed. It reminded me of my cubby hole in Vietnam. But with no air conditioner. And no bathroom, sink, shower or microwave oven. I should have been so lucky.

Hurricane Dolly was out in the Gulf churning toward south Texas. Though my replacement was on duty, on days at least, and I could depart at any time, I chose to ride out the storm. My last EMS flight was July 15, 2008. The call was for a man who had been working underneath his vehicle when one of the jacks gave way and landed on his legs. Many calls in south Texas were for vehicle accidents, but I had launched for rattlesnake bites, bee stings, drownings, and gunshot wounds — and even the aftermath of domestic violence. During these last days, as the storm pushed ever onward, advanced weather conditions prompted me to put the helicopter in the hangar rather than wait around for a call I probably wouldn't take.

The Harlingen base battened down the hatches. Hurricane Dolly made landfall on South Padre Island as a category 1 hurricane July 23. Inland, the wind howled like screaming banshees, the rain frisked and beat against buildings, the windows at the station held, and in the morning, it was sunny and calm, with standing water everywhere. I said goodbye to everyone at the base, wished them well, and finally I was on my way north. I learned later that the storm caused 212,000 customers to lose power, with an estimated 1.3 billion dollars in damages. Gratefully, the hurricane produced no deaths in south Texas. And the hangar within which the aircraft was secured, suffered minor damage as parts of the roof came off exposing sunlight through the opening. But the helicopter was in fine fiddle. I can say that in all my years of flying, except for enemy bullet holes, I never put a scratch on any helicopter I ever flew, or was responsible for.

Thoughts

LONGEVITY AS a helicopter pilot, I always thought, depended on several factors. I wish I could say, however, that my time in Vietnam was where I learned the conservative values that served me so well later. I took chances with the Huey in Vietnam I never would have done with any aircraft I flew in the civilian world. That I flew the Huey beyond its max gross weight limitation almost all the time is a matter of personal remembrance. Troops desperate to leave an LZ will not wait for the pilot to do a weight and balance computation. The D model Huey was woefully underpowered. We learned how to limp the helicopter out of a soggy landing zone (a technique that did serve me well in the civilian world). Our eyes were always glued to the N2 tachometer and the torque gauge. We had to be forever mindful of aircraft ahead and above us, to stay away from the "dirty air" generated by their rotor downwash. Changing positions in formation was always stressful. One miscalculation was all it took to result in a mid-air collision. Flying EMS, we could turn down a flight request for practically any reason, but did so mostly because of weather. In Vietnam, anyone who needed our help was all the reason we needed to crank and go. Rarely could we in good conscience refuse to give assistance. Even knowing the Viet Cong were close by didn't make us falter. Strange the difference between flying helicopters in Vietnam and in the civilian world, especially "flight for life." In the military if you trash a helicopter, especially in war, they just give you another one. In the United States, people may be hurt, they may be dying, but if the weather isn't right, you can't go—your parent company doesn't have unlimited resources.

Accident prevention is a matter of projecting your current action into the future. For example, driving on the highway at 50 mph in clear weather is different than driving 50 mph in foggy pea soup. Driving too fast in fog you can predict an accident. Your toddler reaching for a glass of milk at the edge of the dining room table, you can predict the glass leaving the table, the milk spilling on carpeted floor. It was learned that Kennedy didn't intend to take off from Essex County Airport in Fairfield, New Jersey, after dark. (He was off the ground at 8:38 p.m.) His sister-in-law's work plus traffic delays getting to the airport caused Kennedy to leave much later than planned. A loss of visual reference once over the Atlantic, with confusion reigning in his head, Kennedy didn't project his actions into the future: that an untimely death might result if he didn't turn back to the Rhode Island shoreline with its abundance of ground reference lights.

The aborted Apollo 13 mission was not a matter of projecting the explosion enroute to the moon. It was, however, a matter of projecting what had to be done to get the crew safely home. In the movie, my favorite line is: "Gentlemen, failure is not an option." Look around, where you work, at your home, in your garage, at your hangar. I knew a pilot who started his preflight of the helicopter long before reaching it. He noticed something odd one day about the way the Huey tail rotor assembly looked. He got closer and gazed at it. *Something's wrong.* He called a tech inspector. The TI pondered the way the two tail rotor blades were mounted. Then it hit him. The blades had been installed in reverse, the leading edges going in the wrong direction. You can see a lot from afar, based on what you know is normal.

The abnormal leaped right out at the pilot before he got within a few feet of the aircraft.

In the flight I was assigned at Fort Rucker, one of our instructors had the habit of being the first to the flight line with his students, and the first back in the briefing room at the completion of instruction, so that he could always be home early. I learned that he was so eager to get in the air that he started the aircraft one day without a full load of fuel. He had to shut down and get gas. Out first and back first, I had the impression he was going to get bit, I just didn't know by what. Then one night, all aircraft were called to home base before time was up. There had been an accident at the Troy airport south of Montgomery, Alabama. A helicopter had crashed, the students got out, the instructor was burned alive. It was the very instructor I'm writing about. I can't say that his eagerness to be in the air would lead to an accident, but he seemed oblivious to the idea that *haste makes waste*. The autopsy showed he had ninety percent heart-valve blockage. I had a sense of something bad happening. I guess I wasn't too far wrong.

The space shuttle Challenger disaster (January 28, 1986) directly after launch had been cautioned about, almost predicted. Engineers warned of frigid temperatures and that the O rings could fail. Their vision into the future was dismissed by management. *Accident prevention is projecting actions into the future.*

You can tell a conscientious pilot versus one who is not. He who is not conscientious likes to show off. To impress his passengers, he will do with the aircraft that which is either unsafe or beyond the machine's operating limits. He has a certain braggadocio about him. His ego is small and he is unsure of himself. A conscientious pilot has nothing to prove — to anyone. Not even to himself. A conscientious pilot respects his aircraft. If he treats his machine right, it will treat him right.

I have flown with a lot of other pilots, check airmen, brother pilots. About half I wouldn't want to fly with again. The best pilot (in terms of conscientious congeniality) I ever had the privilege of flying with was an army evaluation instructor who wanted to see me perform after I had been teaching the Huey transition. There were certain maneuvers I still hadn't quite figured out. He put me immediately at ease telling me that he would do the first maneuver and I would do the next one. Then we would critique each other. Under the guise of friendly competition, we learned something from each other. I gained a clearer understanding, for example, of the anti-torque, fixed-pedal emergency and subsequent landing procedure. Regarding the winds and how they affected the tail boom, his simple explanation made perfect sense.

Pilots more practiced should advise those less experienced, rather than showoff or speak glowingly of past exploits.

Situational awareness: what is it? A good example is as you go to your parked car in the driveway, you notice your son's bicycle laying on its side behind the left rear wheel. You move the bicycle before driving away. You are driving down a residential street and you see a bouncing ball come out from between parked cars. What can you assume? That there will be a child close behind. What should you do? Well, first, in a residential neighborhood, you should never exceed the speed limit; in fact, you should go slower in anticipation of a bouncing ball, or someone opening the driver-side car door to exit. If you are rotary-wing qualified and on approach to a confined area LZ, if you happen to see a lone telephone pole in the LZ, you can assume that a wire is probably attached to the pole, the wire coming from somewhere outside the confined area. Else, why the pole? If you aren't sure where to put the aircraft on the ground, think "where do I want the tail rotor to be?" Wherever it is safest to put the tail rotor, think next where to place the landing gear that will have the tail rotor be where you want. I've landed a helicopter on narrow two-lane roads, highways, in barnyards, in open fields, pastures, on rooftop helipads, in mountainous terrain, in parking lots—each location had its own set of hazards. Situational awareness is seeing everything you can before committing to a final descent for landing. My technique for making an approach in a helicopter is first doing a right turn high recon to get a lay of the land. When I knew where the first responders wanted me to put the aircraft, I came to a high hover slightly offset from the point of touchdown, checked my power, and began a slow descent. I even use the anti-torque pedals to redirect the nose of the helicopter so I could see what the instrument panel was hiding from view. I was always prepared to abort were I to note something amiss. Once, I was descending and saw I was kicking up a lot of dust. Before becoming engulfed in a brownout, I merely stopped the descent and added power to climb. The first responders had to find a better place for me to land.

When I drive in highway traffic, I am always glancing in my mirrors—always. When you fly, and the visibility is such that you can see most everywhere outside the cockpit, you cannot be so focused inside the cockpit that you don't look around. One day in Vietnam while the flight of helicopters I was in was shifting the formation, I happened to glance to my left rear (I was in the right seat—the PIC position) and saw another helicopter veering toward mine. My copilot was flying. I took immediate evasive action. I slapped my cyclic control stick hard to the right, the aircraft careened to the right and downward. Those in the formation behind us said that we came within a hair's breadth of mixing rotor blades. Now that is a clear case of situational awareness. *Never leave home without it.*

As I mentioned at the beginning of this book, it was never my intent to be a pilot, but there was something about flying a helicopter that wasn't the same as flying an airplane.

An airplane is something you go somewhere in; a helicopter is something you do something with.

It was the "doing something with" that fascinated me. But a helicopter is just like an airplane once you are in forward flight. Getting off the ground and landing and parking are the tricky parts. If the prop fails or falls off, an airplane will glide. If the rotor system fails or falls off, a helicopter doesn't glide. But an airplane needs level ground and enough of it to land. A helicopter needs nothing more than a clear space big enough to fit.

My first tour in Vietnam was a John Wayne experience. Though I had my near misses and challenges, I never came home with any extra holes, no part of me was missing. Maybe my innocence.

Upon my return to the United States, before a year was up, I volunteered to go back to Vietnam. What happened during my second tour soured me forever. A flight school classmate was shot down and killed flying in a Cobra gunship. His wife requested I be his official military body escort. The funeral was beyond surreal. After the funeral I was scheduled to return to Vietnam. I didn't return. In 1969, Richard Nixon was sworn in as President. He won the election promising to end the war.

Fifty-eight thousand men and women died in Vietnam. To this day, the reason the United States was there is still not clear. But the war allowed me to gain a skill I would have never had otherwise. Some compensation I suppose. I did make good use of that skill: as an army national guard pilot, as an instructor pilot, and as a "flight for life" helicopter pilot.

Looking back on my time as a pilot, as I sit here at the computer composing, I find I miss flying. But I don't miss the stress. I bought X-plane 11 and so I keep my hand at the controls on the computer, armchair flying wherever I want in the world.

Postscript

THIS BOOK is intended to help your thinking. How to keep flying rules and procedures simple. By my reading the FAR/AIM and coupling that with the hours I spent teaching, it was easy to see a path from confusion to coherency. The earth must be visible to not need the flight instruments to control the aircraft. If the instruments are needed, instrument flight rules and procedures are necessary to avoid a collision with obstructions and/or other aircraft. If you are following visual flight rules you must follow basic VFR weather minimums. To be closer to a cloud than is allowed is to be in instrument flight rule weather conditions. There is a hierarchy to controlled airspace. From top to bottom the hierarchy of controlled airspace restricts VFR flight less and less, until within Class G uncontrolled airspace where ATC control of air traffic is non-existent for traffic separation. The purpose of special use airspace is two-fold: to keep non-participating pilots aware and away, and to contain dangerous activities.

Instrument flight procedures are how you fly in the national airspace without regard to VFR weather minimums. A procedure is a "how-to" recipe. How to plan, how to depart, how to navigate enroute, how to arrive, and how to do an instrument approach. An ATC clearance is how one avoids other air traffic. It is also how to avoid obstructions. It is how to stay alive in the national airspace. Flying is ten percent aircraft control and ninety percent thinking. Step-by-step thinking is how to keep your wits in IFR conditions.

I added the pages about EMS flying to give the reader a sense of a helicopter pilot's line of thinking. Countless times I have seen photos and videos of helicopter flight, but it seems that there is never a picture of the pilot(s) or an interview with one to know his thoughts and fears, how he regards his profession. Stunt flying in a helicopter for the entertainment industry is so off the mark that I cannot watch it. The public, I'm certain, has a completely unrealistic picture of helicopter flying.

During the 1968 Tet offensive, we pilots had to ferry replacement troops to  major installations all over Vietnam. Days and days of formation flying, hours and hours at the controls. The pilot *not* at the controls slept. The pilot manipulating the controls *longed* for sleep. I remember never hating being a pilot more than during that time. Whenever I'm around a person who talks nonstop, after a fashion I physically begin to hurt. That's what it was like to fly seemingly nonstop. I recall one time not getting out of my cockpit seat for eight straight hours. When I finally did unstrap and step out, it was to go to the bathroom. My longest flight-hour day was fifteen hours. The average daily flight hours were between seven and nine hours while I was assigned to the 121st Assault Helicopter Company. I chronicled my time in Vietnam in my novel "The Sky Soldiers." Nine months of helicopter flight training is also depicted.

In flying, maybe most pertinent to EMS helicopter piloting, there is what's called "the yellow light" syndrome. As you know regarding traffic signals, there is green, yellow, and red. Green of course means go. Red naturally means stop. But what does yellow mean? Speed up? Slow down? Both? Which is it?

What if your habit is to speed up to get through a yellow light before it turns red? What if your habit is to look so far ahead that when you see a green light you start to slow down in anticipation of it turning yellow? If you speed up to get through a yellow light, that is called "squeezing the oranges." You do that too many times and one day the light will turn red before you figured it would. Then one day you'll run a red light. How many red lights can you run before you plow into someone? Odds are you will have an accident. So constantly running yellow lights is called "the yellow light" syndrome.

In flying EMS, the reason you launch is because a person is having a medical emergency, maybe even life-threatening. You check the weather and it's forecasted green to go. You lift and on the way the forecast starts to fall apart. The visibility doesn't look so promising. If you keep on going, you've snuck past your first yellow light. And you had plenty of time. Farther on, the visibility gets a little fuzzier but you are not giving up. That now is the second yellow light. Now the visibility is starting to look a lot worse. It started out light snow flurries now the flurries are becoming heavier. You continue, but this time yellow turns red before you get through the light. Technically, you just ran a red light. A little farther along and the snow flurries are tapering off. You breathe a sigh of relief. But you are forgetting something. You must, after you pick up the patient, return the same way you came. Now what I say has really happened. The patient is onboard and you begin back the way you came, to the now-called receiving hospital. More than an hour has gone by. The flurries are still out there. The visibility is above company minimums … so all is well. The visibility isn't as good as you'd like but … it's not bad.

When you make it to the hospital, and the crew and patient are out of the aircraft and on their way inside the hospital, you start to think: "Did I keep going when the crew thought I shouldn't? They never said anything. But we did get back okay." I can guarantee you are going to have many flights like that, until you learn to recognize "the yellow light" syndrome.

You can only squeeze through so many yellow lights before you run the critical red light. Those who ran the critical red light are not with us anymore. They are deceased. The yellow light is more than a signal to slow down, it is a signal to turn around before you see red.

I went through driver training for the railroad one time and learned how to react to all the lights. Green means *prepare* to stop. Yellow means *stop*. And red means *you had better be stopped*. I've never forgotten the implications of these sage words.

EMS flying is the most all-encompassing flying I have ever done. During a twelve-hour shift you have not a single clue as to when or where you might have to fly a patient. You are expected to make the quickest decisions ever in your life.

And not a single decision can be wrong. A wrong decision is a fatal decision. EMS helicopter pilots make hundreds of little decisions that make the one big decision. To go or not go? To continue or turn around? To be on the ground or not? When?

Better to be on the ground wishing you were flying,
than in the air flying, wishing you were on the ground.

About the Author

VICTOR BEAVER began his flying career at age nineteen when he attended the U.S. Army warrant officer flight training program in January 1967, graduating September 23, 1967. He was assigned a month later to the 121st Assault Helicopter Company, the "Soc Trang Tigers," deep in the Mekong Delta. He became an aircraft commander at the end of December, after nearly four hundred hours of co-pilot time. During the 1968 Tet Offensive, he was resupplying a district town in the Tra Vinh province when his aircraft received numerous rounds of enemy machinegun fire that permanently grounded his helicopter. After his first tour, he returned to Fort Wolters, Texas, the army's primary helicopter school and was selected to be a tactical training officer. After about four months of overseeing warrant officer candidates and their officer development, he volunteered to return to Vietnam, earlier, perhaps, than he would have been selected to do. He became involved in a test project, evaluating a helicopter fitted with a night-seeing device slaved to the ship's machinegun and rocket system. Then he was faced with a most unfortunate duty, that of official body escort for a flight school classmate shot down in Vietnam while flying in a Cobra gunship. Victor Beaver was slated to return to Vietnam but due to a case of PTSD, he was relieved of this obligation by the flight surgeon.

He attended college in Pueblo, Colorado, became married, then was recalled to active duty to fill the instructor-pilot ranks at Fort Rucker, Alabama, the army's main helicopter training center. After nine years teaching, he left Fort Rucker for a "flight for life" pilot position with Rocky Mountain Helicopters, finally retiring July 2008. His flying career spanned 38 years: seven years active duty, eight years as an army national guard pilot, nine years instructing, and fourteen years flying EMS. In all his years flying, he never had an accident or an incident, put not one scratch on any helicopter he ever commanded—except for bullet holes on more than a few occasions in Vietnam. He lives with his wife Linda in their 5th wheel RV traveling between Colorado, Springfield, Missouri, and the Rio Grande valley.

Victor R. Beaver

He is the author of the novel, "The Sky Soldiers," a 16-month-long saga of flying helicopters in Vietnam, for sale on Amazon.com and Barnes & Noble.com.

Acknowledgements

USUALLY AN author thanks numerous people who helped with the publication of a book. I would like to thank those long-established writers who taught me what good writing is and how to recognize it.

- John Steinbeck, author of *East of Eden, Grapes of Wrath,* and *Travels with Charlie*
- Ernest Gann, author of *Fate is the Hunter, Benjamin Lawless,* and *Band of Brothers*
- Edward Abbey, author of *Desert Solitaire, Black Sun, The Monkey Wrench Gang,* and *Fire on the Mountain*
- James Michener, author of *Caravans, Hawaii, The Source, The Covenant,* and so many, many more
- Henry David Thoreau, author of *Walden, Life in the Woods,* and *On the Duty of Civil Disobedience*
- Leon Uris, author of *Battle Cry, Exodus, Mila 18,* and *Armageddon*
- Elmer Kelton, author of one book in particular *The Wolf and the Buffalo*
- Ayn Rand, author of *We The Living, The Fountainhead, Atlas Shrugged, The Romantic Manifesto,* and *Introduction to Objectivist Epistemology*
- Nevil Shute, author of numerous books, my favorites being *A Town Like Alice, No Highway, Most Secret, Trustee from the Tool Room, Round the Bend, The Rainbow and the Rose,* and *On the Beach*
- George Orwell, author of *1984*
- Aldous Huxley, author of *Brave New World* and *Brave New World Revisited*
- and Nelson DeMille, author of *The Gold Coast, Up Country,* and *Night Fall*

I've read thousands of books, and I always study the comma, the most difficult punctuation mark to get exactly right. But I'm learning.

To be an accomplished writer one must study and attempt to emulate good writing. And one must write often, one must edit and revise and revise again, and proof read and revise some more, until nothing more can be assumed to make the writing better. There must come a stopping point. And still it won't be perfect.

I thank my wife Linda Nija Nations for her support and encouragement. And my mother Marcelene L. Beaver, always willing to provide financial support. And I thank the United States government for its publication of the FAR/AIM which I tried my best to cipher into relative coherency. May its changes forever aim toward less confusion and toward more collision avoidance procedures.

— Victor R. Beaver, author

Excerpt from "The Sky Soldiers"

At San Francisco International Airport, the western skies were showing the very last of the day's light. With a folded American flag under his right arm, Kip Slater stood on the concrete surface of the loading ramp and watched the loading crew drive forward bearing Leo's casket. When the vehicle, designed to raise heavy objects up until level with the cargo opening of the plane, had stopped, Kip went and asked that one of the operators help him spread the flag to cover the casket. A young man, eighteen, his face expressionless, stepped forward. Kip handed him one end and the two carefully unfolded the red white and blue cloth and gently laid the Stars and Stripes over the casket. After it was secured. Kip stepped back. Choking back tears, he slowly raised his right arm; he held the salute a heartbeat longer than customary; then he let his arm come slowly down.

Kip went and stood at the bottom of the stairs that led back into the terminal waiting area. He watched the men raise the casket to the cargo opening. As the casket went into the ship's hold, he happened to glance to his left. On the concrete surface, he saw a pair of mourning doves stepping about, chortling softly. He peered at them for a moment; then, without apparent cause or reason, they burst into flight. Kip saw them, their wings fluttering, fly past the cargo opening; then were gone in the deep, dark blue night.

The cargo door remained open. Kip turned, glanced at the door at the top of the stairs leading to the terminal, and then looked back at the plane, at the open cargo door. He took a step and then remembered the folded piece of paper and on it the poem written by Thoreau, given to Leo by his mother. Leo had left it on his cot in the gun platoon tent. Kip removed his billfold, took out the paper and unfolded it.

... And the long afterglow gives light,
And the damask curtains glow along the
Western window
And now the first star is lit,
And I go home ...

The cargo door closed. Kip saw a lone star twinkling overhead. He took a slow breath. "Come on, Leo ... It's time to go home."

I can be reached by email: pilotbeaver@hotmail.com or by cell phone: (417) 335-1394. I welcome any and all suggestions or comments.

Afterthoughts

IT IS my sincere hope that this book made a dent. Now that I am no longer flying there is still a part of me that would like to make a difference, especially regarding helicopter flying. Flight instructing in a UH-1 Huey helicopter was rewarding and launching on a medical flight was important. Which always prompted me to declare: "And they pay me to do this!"

EMS helicopter flying is a dangerous game. But it is not inherently dangerous, "... It is only unforgiving of human error."

My mantra about whether to launch on a medical flight was: "If the atmospheric conditions aren't right ... tis better that the patient go by ground ambulance than for me to have him stuck out in the middle of nowhere because I had to abort the flight."

Was the flight program or hospital out potential revenue? Certainly. But what about the loss of a two-million-dollar or a three-million-dollar aircraft? And lawsuits? An EMS accident is likely a more legitimate cause for a lawsuit than most.

I can testify to a truth: an EMS helicopter that never goes anywhere or does anything is an expense not worth having. An EMS flight program that attempts to "save" every patient is not worth the expense, either. A "flight for life" program does not "save lives." At best it reduces morbidity (the effects of illness or injury) — meaning the quality of life is probably assured by using a helicopter. There is no quality of life if a patient goes down with the crew and is killed because of the mistaken idea that the only way a patient can get to the hospital is by air ambulance.

I shall relate a flight I had one night from Springfield, Missouri, to Seneca, Missouri, a little town right on the Oklahoma state line just south of Joplin. On state highway 43 there had been an accident. I was called, I checked the weather, and I accepted the flight. The accident site was less than 18 miles from the nearest hospital in Joplin. The distance to the scene of the accident from Cox South was about 65 miles. Given a no wind condition, the flight (at 120 mph) would normally take about 30 minutes. Once I was enroute, my GPS indicated that my groundspeed was around 60 mph due to a very strong headwind. At that rate it would take me over an hour to arrive at the scene. I relayed my time enroute to the ambulance crew and first responders and they said keep coming. Normally, once a scene is arrived at, it takes another ten, fifteen, maybe twenty minutes at most to load the patient and go. I knew where Seneca was, I knew how close the patient was to the nearest hospital in Joplin, and I knew that the patient would be better off going by ground ambulance that short distance. They insisted I keep coming. So, I continued slugging my way in an MBB BO 105 helicopter to the scene. I don't know if I need to explain this any further. The use of the helicopter was totally ludicrous. But they had set the landing zone up, the firefighters were there to keep traffic at bay, and because of all this effort it was imperative that the helicopter be used.

I had another flight one night to a scene location near Mansfield, Missouri, thirty-five miles east of Springfield. A ninety-four-year-old woman was suffering a heart attack. Protocol demanded that a helicopter be used. So, I went. I got her to St. Johns Hospital. The medical crew told me during the flight that the woman was not on any prescription meds, which was remarkable for her age. She died peaceably that morning in the hospital. Her family was stuck with a monstrous bill for the flight. The ground ambulance crew should have driven her in.

Flight crews don't turn down flights due to lack of feasibility. Or cost. Or generally for any reason other than weather. But notice that between these two scenarios how *unavailable* the helicopter was for other equally serious medical problems. The adage: "Better safe than sorry" can likely be applied to using a helicopter for transport: "Better to use the helicopter and not be chastised than not use it and certainly be chastised."

One last scenario. Northwest of Joplin there had been a terrible multi-car pileup involving multiple EMS helicopters. Several people were killed and those still alive were taken to area hospitals. The woman I picked up seemed perfectly fine. The crew really couldn't find much wrong with her but because the accident had generated at least one death, she was onboard to make sure she had no undetected internal injuries. I even talked to her on the flight. She seemed happy, maybe because it was her first time in a helicopter. She died at KU Med Center in Kansas City that night.

Be on the lookout for my next book: "Flight for Life: An Introduction to EMS Helicopter Flying." An in-depth synopsis.

I believe the best way to get familiar with the FAR/AIM is to do a scavenger hunt. Not every question I pose is critical. But if you bother to look for the answers to *every* question, I guarantee you'll stumble onto something interesting to learn more about. Don't believe for a minute that every detail you digest will be outdated a month or two later. For example, not much has changed regarding two-way radio failure. You can most definitely rely on the idea that when you are cleared for an approach, the missed approach procedure is also included. And that the missed approach holding fix is your official clearance limit. Seriously, how can it be otherwise?

Questions & Answers

(Answers found in *your* current AIM.)

1. Nondirectional radio beacons (NDBs) are subject to [atmospheric] disturbances, as well as interference from distant stations, especially at night, that may result in erroneous bearing information which affect the ADF receiver. Name some of the disturbances and how the pilot might guard against relying on false information.
2. What is the only positive method of identifying a VOR?
3. How does the pilot know when a VOR facility is undergoing maintenance?
4. How is a VOR navigation transmitter different from a nondirectional radio beacon (NDB)?
5. What is a VOT? What is the permitted frequency of the VOT? What does +/- 4 degrees refer to? What does +/- 6 degrees refer to?
6. What is the service volume of a T (Terminal) VOR? Of an L (Low Altitude) VOR? Of an H (High Altitude) VOR?
7. What is the service volume of a compass locator?
8. There are three marker beacons typically associated with an ILS instrument approach. Name the usage of each marker beacon.
9. ILS course distortion. What might be the cause and how is it protected against?
10. Regarding alternate airport considerations, is a GPS instrument approach procedure allowed for letdown?
11. A page to denote designated mountainous areas is for what purpose?
12. Find the page where it states that when cleared for an instrument approach, a clearance to perform the missed approach procedure is implied. Verbatim from the AIM: "A clearance for an instrument approach procedure *includes* a clearance to fly the published missed approach procedure, unless otherwise instructed by ATC."
13. Re: question #12, yes or no, does this imply that the official clearance limit, if a landing cannot be made, is the missed approach *holding* fix?
14. What phraseology does ATC use to grant permission to enter Class C airspace?
15. What are the obstacle clearance requirements for IFR flight in Class G (uncontrolled) airspace in non-mountainous terrain?
16. What is the pilot's responsibility when approaching a clearance limit? The controller's responsibility?

17. How does a pilot answer a yes or no question posed by ATC? Is it roger? Yay or nay? Yes or no? Affirmative or negative? And why the last? There is no reasoning given in the AIM, but take a guess.

18. When timed approaches from a holding fix are in progress, may a pilot, upon receipt of approach clearance, perform the depicted procedure turn? Why not?

19. What is the advantage of a teardrop procedure or penetration turn when used for course reversal as depicted on an approach plate?

20. In that Class D airspace extends upward from the surface to 2,500 feet above the airport elevation (charted in MSL), may a VFR pilot in VFR conditions overfly the airport at or above the charted MSL altitude without radio communications with the tower operator? Generally, what class of airspace will the VFR pilot be in?

21. If a NAVAID does not have voice capability, how is it depicted? What is the advantage of voice capability?

22. What is a changeover point (COP) and how is it used?

23. When are traffic advisories provided by ATC?

24. If an aircraft is transponder equipped, what transponder code should be entered for VFR operations and why?

25. Is the airspace above FL 600 Class E airspace?

26. When ATC observing his radar scope advises you of a target at your 3 o'clock position, is it based on your aircraft heading or ground track?

27. What is the difference between the terms Distress and Urgency to signal to ATC that you are experiencing an inflight difficulty?

28. During two-way radio failure how should your transponder be used?

29. Air traffic control radar is different than weather radar. Explain the difference.

30. What is the VHF emergency frequency? UHF? May you use the emergency frequency to keep an ongoing conversation with ATC?

31. What does CTAF stand for? Under what circumstances is it used? Why should it be used?

32. When should the phonetic alphabet be used when referring to your call sign?

33. There is an entire advisory section in the FAR/AIM regarding practice instrument approaches. What criteria does ATC use to accommodate those pilots who wish to do practice IAPs?

34. When an ATC generated amended clearance is issued is it appropriate for ATC to simultaneously give a lengthy explanation why the amendment? May the pilot request the reasoning behind the amendment?

35. A heavy aircraft has just lifted from the takeoff runway, the same runway you are to depart from. How do you avoid his wake turbulence?

36. When conducting a direct flight (not using established routes or airways), which fixes automatically become compulsory reporting points?

37. When may an IFR flight plan be canceled?

38. What are some of the limitations of a STAR (standard arrival route procedure)?

39. When radar is used to guide aircraft onto the final approach course (called vectors to final), when approach clearance is given, is the controller required to state "cleared straight-in?"

40. Is there an odd/even cruising altitude "rule" for enroute VFR flight? Why should it be used?

41. When are AGL and MSL equal? Does it depend on barometric pressure?

42. Is it possible to receive "false" glideslope information? How?

43. Why should you file a VFR flight plan, even if you are to remain within sight of your base airport?

44. Why should pilots avoid unexpected maneuvers in the airport traffic pattern?

45. What is a microburst? When is it most detrimental to aircraft?

46. May the landing light be used on approach to an airport during daylight?

47. Special VFR operations by fixed-wing aircraft are prohibited between sunset and sunrise unless what criteria are met by the pilot and the aircraft?

48. By what distance should a pilot avoid any type of thunderstorm activity?

49. You are in the clouds. How might you detect icing conditions earlier than falling out of the sky because your aircraft is no longer aerodynamically sound?

50. To operate VFR within a 60-nautical mile radius of the Washington, D.C. VOR/DME, is there special awareness training required? What are the exceptions?

51. What are the fuel requirements for flight in IFR conditions?

52. Explain the VOR equipment check for IFR operations.

53. What is the obstacle clearance requirement(s) for IFR flight in Class G (uncontrolled) airspace in mountainous terrain?

54. What actions must be taken by the pilot and ATC to compensate for GPS interruptions?

55. Using VASI, visual glideslope indicators, what is the normal glide path angle? What is the caution for VASI glide path angles of more than 3.5°? A VASI glide path angle of 4.5° is used for what purpose?

56. What color are runway edge lights? What color are taxiway edge lights?

57. Beginning at what height must a tower be lit?

58. What special precautions must be taken when taxiing on the airport surface in dense fog?

59. What airspace areas are listed as regulatory? What airspace areas are listed as nonregulatory?

60. To qualify for surface Class E airspace status, the airport must have what feature?

61. True or false. The 700-foot/1,200-foot AGL Class E airspace transition areas remain in effect continuously, regardless of airport operating hours or surface area status. What does this have to do with Basic VFR?

62. What is the purpose of establishing a temporary flight restrictions (TFA) area?

63. Explain VFR corridors through certain Class B airspace areas?

64. What is a stuck mic? If your mic is stuck, how would you know it?

65. How is an ELT activated? Do you need to crash land for it to activate?

66. How are helicopters operated at a tower-controlled airport? Provided ground operations and conditions permit, is helicopter *air taxi* the preferred ground movement on the airport surface?

67. What are the options when "cleared for the option" at a tower-controlled airport?

68. When an immediate deviation from the elements of a route clearance is performed for urgent or emergency reasons, how soon should the pilot inform ATC?

69. Is it the pilot's responsibility to accept or refuse an ATC clearance as issued? What then must the pilot request?

70. If there are no published missed approach procedures depicted on an instrument approach plate, what is the pilot expected to do? What must ATC do?

71. What is the useful range of the two PAR antennas?

72. True or false, a *bearing* is an indication FROM and a *course* is an indication TO. To establish your position from a NAVAID, you receive a bearing *from* it. To proceed to a NAVAID, you follow a course *to* it.

73. What is the difference between an ATC request to "expedite climb" or "climb at pilot's discretion?"

74. Typically, ATC will clear a pilot to do a specific instrument approach. If ATC merely states: "Cleared for approach," what does it imply by not naming the approach?

75. What is a no-gyro approach? Why is it used?

76. There is a paragraph in the FAR/AIM describing Landing Priority. Does local traffic have landing priority over an IFR aircraft? Or vice versa?
77. What is the emergency transponder squawk code? For lost communications? For hi-jacking?
78. What is the difference between a SIGMET, a CONVECTIVE SIGMET, and an AIRMET?
79. What are the characteristics of a microburst?
80. What weather phenomena are associated with thunderstorms?
81. The accuracy of aircraft altimeters is subject to what factors?
82. Cold, dry air masses may produce barometric pressures in excess of 31.00 inches of mercury. How is your aircraft altimeter affected? If you can't reset your altimeter to a value higher than 31.00 inches of mercury, will you be higher or lower than you are intended to be?
83. If wingtip vortices are a problem on takeoff, how might it affect your aircraft once airborne below 1,000 feet AGL?
84. The size of an aircraft will generate a proportional level of wingtip vortices. Find in the AIM where size comparisons require appropriate distances to preclude the lessoning effects of wake turbulence.
85. Bird strike risk is highest during what months?
86. What are the ten most frequent cause factors of general aviation accidents that involve the pilot-in-command?
87. In the FAR/AIM there is a page and a half devoted to mountain flying. One of my instrument students became not only instrument rated but became an instrument flight examiner. He bought an airplane, was flying in the mountains of Colorado, and was killed while trying to negotiate a turn in a box canyon. It was determined that he allowed his aircraft to stall in the turn. Does turning increase or reduce stall speed?
88. What is precipitation static?
89. What is hypoxia?
90. How can emotional stress affect your ability to fly safely?
91. Explain the different illusions that can be experienced in flight.
92. When scanning for other aircraft in your vicinity, or the tops of tall radio towers that might present a collision hazard, where do you look? Below the horizon? Above the horizon? Or ever so slightly above the horizon?
93. What do the following acronyms represent: MOCA, MEA, MCA, MRA, MTA, MVA, MDA?
94. One of my favorite acronyms is VDP. Every non-precision approach procedure should have a calculated or identifiable visual descent point, as a prewarning that a missed approach is likely. Do you agree?

95. What is air density and what is density altitude and what are the effects of density altitude?
96. In holding are right turns standard or non-standard?
97. What is the current cost of the FAR/AIM?
98. Would it be worth it to purchase X-plane 11 and program visibility values less than 5 miles to see what flying at night would be like? And during the day?
99. What is smog? Should it be classed as an atmospheric condition that limits visibility? The higher you fly in hazy or smoggy conditions, the less able you are to see the ground. At night it is worse. True or false?
100. Was this book worth the money spent?

If God had meant Man to fly,
He would have born him wings.
If God had not meant Man to fly,
Man would not have been created
By God.

The most lyrical book I have ever had the privilege to read was "Fate in the Hunter," by Ernest Gann. It is a book that inspires flight, where man and machine are as one. You will not be disappointed.

—Victor R. Beaver